AMERICA'S NATIONAL SECURITY ARCHITECTURE: REBUILDING THE FOUNDATION

EDITED BY NICHOLAS BURNS AND JONATHON PRICE

CONTRIBUTORS INCLUDE:

Graham Allision; Zoë Baird; Robert D. Blackwill; Nicholas E
James Cartwright; John Dowdy; Peter Feaver; Niall Fergu
Stephen Hadley; Jennifer M. Harris; Christopher Kirchh
Jane Holl Lute; Joseph S. Nye; Thomas Pritzker; Kirk Rieck
John Sawers; Julianne Smith; James Steinberg; Douglas S
Dov Zakheim; Leah Joy Zell

aspen strategy group

Acknowledgements

Nicholas Burns
Director
Aspen Strategy Group

Jonathon Price
Deputy Director
Aspen Strategy Group

Just months before a new administration would step into the White House, the Aspen Strategy Group convened in Aspen, Colorado, to focus on reforming the U.S. government's national security system to account for the myriad of challenges the United States will face in the coming years. This publication contains a collection of policy papers written by experts who served in many facets of the U.S. government and private sector, from trade and business to defense and national security. These experts guided our discussion in Aspen, highlighting a multitude of challenges and providing several recommendations for the U.S. government moving forward—which you can read in the following pages. Participants at the Strategy Group meeting included a bipartisan group of ASG members and invited guests, from current and former government officials to journalists and private sector leaders.

The Aspen Strategy Group would not be able to convene such a group without the generous support of our partners. The organizations and individuals who invest in our mission enable us to convene an open and bipartisan dialogue on crucial topics in U.S. national security and foreign policy. We are enormously grateful to Mr. Robert Abernethy, McKinsey and Company, Mr. Howard Cox, Markle Foundation, Pritzker Family Foundation, Segal Family Foundation, Stanton Foundation, John Anson Kittredge Educational Fund, Mr. Simon Pinniger and Ms. Carolyne Roehm, Mr. Robert Rosenkranz and Dr. Alexandra Monroe, and Ms. Leah Joy Zell.

To transform this collection of papers into the volume you now hold, we are indebted to Gayle Bennett, who proofread and edited this publication; Steve Johnson, who designed the cover, and Sogand Sepassi, who designed the interior layout. Our Brent Scowcroft Fellows—Daniel Ku, Calli Obern, and Carolina Ponzeto—spent many hours reviewing this manuscript to ensure its quality; we are grateful for their invaluable assistance and look forward to following their careers.

Finally, we must recognize the end of an era. At our meeting this August, our longtime friend and co-chair, Brent Scowcroft, transitioned to chair emeritus. Brent was present at the creation of this group and laid the foundation for all the work the Aspen Strategy Group continues to do. Beyond his well-known public service as national security advisor to two presidents, and his integral role in ending the Cold War peacefully and reshaping Europe, he is the epitome of a public servant. The ASG has been well served by Brent's leadership and three-decade involvement, helping ASG foster bipartisan and frank dialogue on key issues facing the United States and the world. We are enormously grateful and privileged to have benefited from his tenure, and we look forward to welcoming him back to Aspen in his new role soon.

Contents

Part 3
THE MACHINERY OF THE U.S. GOVERNMENT

Part 4
MODERNIZING AMERICA'S NATIONAL SECURITY TOOLS

Part 5

SUMMARY AND CONCLUDING THOUGHTS

Preface

Nicholas Burns
Director, Aspen Strategy Group
Goodman Family Professor of the
Practice of Diplomacy and International Relations
Harvard University

Joseph S. Nye, Jr.
Co-chair, Aspen Strategy Group
University Distinguished Service Professor
Harvard University

Since the end of the Second World War, the United States has been the premier global power. Our modern presidents from Harry Truman to Barack Obama have coordinated that power in the White House principally through the National Security Council (NSC). The NSC was created in 1947, along with the Department of Defense and the CIA, to modernize the way Americans made foreign and defense policy after the crucible of World War II and as the Cold War was just starting.

Now, seven decades later, many believe the new U.S. administration led by Hillary Clinton should launch a new set of reforms to modernize how twenty-first century Americans debate and decide policy in a Washington changed significantly by 9/11, the wars in Iraq and Afghanistan, transnational global issues, cyber challenges, and renewed great power rivalries with China and Russia.

This was the central conclusion of the members of the non-partisan Aspen Strategy Group when we met to discuss the broad subject of policymaking in Washington during our annual summer meeting in Aspen, Colorado in 2016. During four days of meetings, we debated how the vast and complex national security system in Washington should be reformed, restructured and made more effective for the new administration.

Most of the members of our group—former and current government officials, academics, foundation presidents, business leaders and journalists—have spent lifetimes in and out of government in our major federal agencies, the White House, and Congress, closely observing the policy process.

For many, the best model for how an administration should arrange its decision-making process was the presidency of George H.W. Bush. General Brent Scowcroft, Bush's national security advisor (and one of the founders of our group) is widely viewed as one of the most effective people who has ever held that job.

Scowcroft's NSC, on which one of us (Burns) served, was significantly smaller than that of President Obama. Scowcroft was close to President Bush and worked well with Secretary of State James A. Baker III and Secretary of Defense Dick Cheney. He also presided over a policy process that resulted in significant and even historic successes, including the key U.S. role in German unification in 1990, the skillful manner in which Bush handled the end of the Cold War and the demise of the Soviet Union in 1991, and the U.S. coalition's victory over Saddam Hussein in Kuwait that same year. Whenever reform of the NSC is discussed today, scholars and policymakers alike invariably conclude that replicating the Scowcroft model and the smaller, more cohesive and less layered National Security Council of his time would be the wisest course of action.

The reality is, however, that the challenges facing the next American administration in January 2017 will be substantially different from those of the early 1990s. With today's constant threat of terrorism, the advent of cyber challenges against the American government and the private sector and the deployment of American military forces in the Middle East, Africa, Asia, and Europe, there is a reason why the NSC staff has more than tripled in the quarter century since the end of the Cold War. While most agree that the size of the NSC staff should be reduced to more manageable levels, there are good reasons why a staff of several hundred people should work at the nerve center of the American government in this complex era.

This book features essays written on the broad subject of how the United States can build a more streamlined, integrated, and effective national security machinery for the decade ahead.

Specifically, exactly how should the next president reform the national security system? What kind of technology acquisitions, training, and doctrinal changes must we make to create a government that can act in a world dominated by social media and instantaneous communication?

The essays in this book range from the urgent—immediate reform of the NSC structure—to the long term—establishing an NSC strategy group to inform long term policy with lessons from the past.

One of the takeaways that most participants agreed upon at the Aspen conference is that our presidents get the national security system they want and deserve. Presidents have a right to put their personal imprint on their staff structure so that it works best for them.

Nonetheless, our group coalesced around a set of practical ideas that should apply to any president. Many believed a strong president should delegate to strong cabinet secretaries, particularly at the two agencies that are at the core of our national security system—the State and Defense Departments. There was a general consensus that the new administration should place much greater emphasis in building America's economic power and in bringing the secretaries of Treasury, Commerce, and Energy into much closer integration with the State and Defense Departments.

We debated the frequent use of the military since 9/11 with many participants arguing for a policy of making diplomacy our first impulse and using the military as a last resort. We also felt that more could be done to coordinate the instruments of American soft power.

There was also agreement that staying ahead of the technology curve would be critical to sustain America's qualitative military edge over all of its potential rivals. In this sense, there was strong interest in the Pentagon's third offset strategy—a multi-year, multi-billion dollar effort to achieve engineering and technology breakthroughs for our military forces over the next generation.

In many ways this book provides a roadmap to the future of American power in a complex and challenging global landscape.

We believe that the great value of our group is its commitment to the future of our country and our ability to work across party lines for an active, leading global role for the United States in the decades ahead.

Part

"*The shock of Pearl Harbor led to the creation of a network of national security institutions designed around two questions: Where is the threat? and Who is the enemy? This Pearl Harbor system served its purpose during the Cold War, but since that time the costs associated with this narrow and reactive approach to foreign policy formulation have outweighed the benefits.*"

—DOUGLAS STUART

The Eighth Annual Ernest May Memorial Lecture
The Pearl Harbor System at 75

Douglas Stuart
Stuart Chair in International Studies
Dickinson College

Editor's Note: Douglas Stuart presented the annual Ernest R. May Memorial Lecture at the Aspen Strategy Group's August 2016 Summer Workshop in Aspen, Colorado. The following is a paper written based on his remarks at the meeting. The Ernest May Memorial Lecture is named for Ernest May, an international relations historian and Harvard John F. Kennedy School of Government professor, who passed away in 2009. ASG developed the lecture series to honor Professor May's celebrated lectures.

I am very honored to have my name linked to Professor Ernest May, who personified the engaged academic. One of Professor May's most important insights was that, whether one is a scholar attempting to explain a specific foreign policy decision or a policy maker engaged in the formulation of foreign policy, it helps to think of time as a stream—in which carefully selected lessons from the past inform the discussion of current issues and help shape plans for the future.[1] But Professor May would also have been the first to admit that this is easier said than done. One big problem that both analysts and policy makers confront when they attempt to derive lessons from the past is deciding how far back one needs to go to make sense of any contemporary situation. We might call this the challenge of infinite regress. How far back do we have to go to explain the Obama administration's pivot to Asia? To the debates surrounding the Truman administration's decision to create a network of military alliances in the Pacific in 1951? To Teddy Roosevelt's deployment of the Great White Fleet in 1907? To the geostrategic arguments of Admiral Mahan in favor of the Open Door to Asia in the late nineteenth century?

There have been a few instances in American history, however, where there is no doubt about how far back we need to go, because a specific event or decision clearly served as the starting point for a new era in U.S. foreign policy. One such event was the Japanese surprise attack on Pearl Harbor in 1941. This single incident set in motion a series of debates and investigations—including 25,000 pages of congressional testimony—which culminated in the development of a new network of policy-making institutions. More importantly, Pearl Harbor changed the way Americans thought about their place in the world by replacing the concept of National Interest, which had served as the basis for U.S. foreign policy since the founding of the Republic, with the concept of National Security.[2]

The articulation and management of the national interest was the responsibility of the Department of State for over 150 years. State was the first executive branch agency created by the new Republic, and serving as secretary of state was the most direct path to the White House between 1789 and the Civil War. Throughout the nineteenth century and up until World War II, secretaries of state managed what Steven Ambrose and Douglas Brinkley have called America's "rise to globalism" by sophisticated diplomacy that privileged American economic interests and exploited the nation's geographic location in order to be selective about foreign entanglements.[3] State also benefited from the nation's suspicion of a large standing military during peacetime, which made it difficult for the Departments of War and Navy to challenge the State Department's dominance of the policy-making process. At times, the State Department's inclination to formulate foreign policy without consulting the armed services was irresponsible. Professor May reminds us that in 1919, while he was serving as assistant secretary of the Navy, Franklin Roosevelt tried to remedy this situation by proposing the creation of an agency that would facilitate cooperation between State and the Army and Navy, but his proposal was not even acknowledged by Foggy Bottom.[4]

By the 1930s, many influential academics and policy makers were expressing dissatisfaction with the concept of national interest as a guide to foreign policy.[5] They tended to make three arguments. First, that many immigrants were manipulating the concept of national interest so that it actually served the interests of the nations from which they had emigrated. Second, that business and labor organizations were using their economic and political power to trick the American people into believing that their narrow and particular interests were actually the national interest. Finally, that Woodrow Wilson had conflated his interest in supranational governance with the national interest, leading us into a war that gave us nothing more than "death, debt and George M. Cohan."[6] These arguments all contributed to the pervasive isolationist mood during the interwar period, but by 1941, there was still no consensus about what concept should replace national interest as a guide to American foreign policy.[7]

Pearl Harbor provided the American people with an alternative to the concept of national interest, based upon five lessons.

1. That technological developments—most notably, improvements in the range and lethality of airplanes—meant, as one expert put it, that "delusions of defensive invulnerability are fairy tales...."[8]

2. That the perfidy and innate aggressiveness of totalitarian governments made the global defense and advancement of democracy a national security concern.

3. That there was a need for a globalized American military presence and mechanisms designed to give military leaders a permanent, direct, and influential role in the formulation of U.S. foreign policies.

4. That there was a need for permanent globalized intelligence-gathering.

5. That there was a need for new institutions and procedures for high-level consultation and decision-making in the service of national security.

These lessons not only helped establish national security as the alternative to national interest, they also helped create the standard against which future national security policies were to be judged—**Preparedness**. The U.S. must never again be "sucker punched" by another nation. To avoid another Pearl Harbor, America would have to permanently maintain what Thomas Hobbes called "the posture of gladiators, having their weapons pointing and their eyes fixed on one another."[9] This is a difficult posture for any nation to sustain, but it is particularly hard, and problematic, for a democracy with a history of selective engagement in world affairs.

It is also worth reminding ourselves that the national preoccupation with preparedness was in place two years before the United States became focused on the Soviet threat. If the two wartime allies had somehow been able to resolve their differences in 1945, the United States would probably still have been looking for ways to preserve a globalized military presence and a worldwide intelligence network after World War II, in the service of preparedness. Once anti-communism took hold, it eclipsed—but did not eliminate—the more general concern about no more Pearl Harbors. That concern was still in place, and ready to reassert itself as a guide to U.S. foreign policy, after the Berlin Wall came down.

Although support for globalized preparedness was nearly universal after World War II, the Truman administration soon discovered there was considerable room for disagreement about how to achieve this goal. New institutions were certainly needed, but what should they look like?

During World War II, Franklin Roosevelt developed some institutions and procedures that served as postwar models. The Office of Strategic Services (OSS) was tasked with the collection of intelligence and acts of sabotage. The Joint Chiefs of Staff (JCS), headed by a chief of staff to the commander in chief, was established to facilitate cooperation between the heads of the Army, Navy, Army Air Forces. The most important innovation was the State, War, Navy Coordinating Committee (SWNCC), which was created in the latter stages of the war to bring together representatives of the State Department, the Army, and the Navy to develop plans for postwar issues, such as the occupation of Germany and Japan. The frustrations that the State Department experienced in SWNCC presaged the problems of marginalization that have plagued Foggy Bottom since World War II.

By the time Harry Truman took office in 1945, he had developed his own very strong opinions about what was needed to insure American preparedness. The top priority had to be armed forces unification, so that future presidents would have "one team, with all the reins in one hand."[10] He was convinced that Pearl Harbor was in large part attributable to failures of communication and coordination between the Army and Navy—failures that had also undermined the nation's ability to develop and pursue a coherent grand strategy during the war. The leaders of the Army supported the call for armed forces unification, in part because they agreed with the president that it would make it easier for the two services to work together and in part because they saw unification as a way to mitigate the negative impact of postwar budget cuts. As Army Chief of Staff George Marshall noted, his service was always disadvantaged in peacetime in its competition for scarce resources with what he called the more "photogenic" Navy—a situation that would only get worse if the even more photogenic Air Force became an independent military service.[11]

Truman's call for unification was strongly opposed by the Navy, and in particular by Secretary of the Navy James Forrestal. But the secretary realized that his service would not be able to resist unification if the American people and Congress saw its opposition as nothing more than a knee-jerk rejection of the president's call for reform. The Navy needed a counter-argument, and over the summer of 1945 it began to hammer out an alternative vision of a network of institutions to serve the daunting demands of preparedness. Over the next two years, the Navy and its supporters in Congress fought with Truman over competing plans, until an exhausted president finally gave in and approved most of the Navy's plan. Although Truman was too much of a politician to admit it, he had lost the battle for what he considered to be one of his most important priorities.

The influence of the Pearl Harbor attack on the debates that culminated in the 1947 National Security Act (NSA) cannot be overestimated. In fact, it is not an exaggeration to describe the network of national security institutions created in the shadow of the Japanese surprise attack as the "Pearl Harbor system." In spite of the fact that the legislation was the result of a tactical move by the Navy to block armed forces unification, the finished product was an extraordinary example of bipartisan negotiation. The massive piece of omnibus legislation created seven new federal agencies, including a new Air Force, and gave the Joint Chiefs of Staff statutory identity. It would be impossible for Washington to pass anything similar today.

The new network of national security institutions created by the 1947 Act was designed to accomplish three things: institutionalized cooperation at the highest levels of government, the generation and dissemination of policy-relevant intelligence, and improvements in the American military's ability to deter potential aggressors and transition to warfare in the event that deterrence failed.

The three most important institutions created by this legislation were the National Security Council (NSC), the Central Intelligence Agency (CIA), and the National Military Establishment (NME), which became the Department of Defense in 1949. The NSC was envisioned as the "keystone in the arch" of this ambitious network of institutions. Although he ultimately approved of the creation of this institution, Truman was concerned that the NSC would function as a "second cabinet" and attempt to influence, rather than inform, his decisions. State Department representatives also warned the president about the risk that the armed forces would be overrepresented in the NSC and dominate its deliberations—the so-called "capture" problem. Military leaders, meanwhile, worried that a defensive State Department would attempt to paralyze NSC discussions and, as they put it, "castrate its effectiveness."[12] In light of these concerns, the president used the NSC infrequently at first, but he became more dependent on it after the U.S. became trapped in Korea.

It was left to Eisenhower to fully develop the NSC as an institution. In his management of the NSC, Eisenhower confronted most of the questions that have been addressed by every president since then. How big should the NSC be? How involved should it be in the monitoring or management of policies once a decision has been made? And what role should a national security advisor play as the gatekeeper between the NSC and the White House? Eisenhower also had to deal with a Congress which, although it accepted in principle the argument that the NSC was the president's "creature," occasionally felt compelled to criticize the president's management of the Council. The lesson for subsequent presidents was that if an administration's foreign policies became unpopular, Congress would be tempted to link the product to the process and begin to intrude in the workings of the Council.[13]

According to the 1947 NSA, the CIA was expected to serve as the "grist" for the NSC's "mill." To accomplish this role, the director of central intelligence (DCI) was authorized to inspect the materials generated by the other intelligence agencies. But the section of legislation relating to the CIA fulfilled Napoleon's standard for a good constitution—it was short and vague. The legislation was particularly ambiguous about the DCI's authority as "the president's chief intelligence officer."[14] John Ranelagh notes that, in theory, this gave the DCI "oversight of all intelligence activities of the U.S. government," but the other big players in the intelligence community took advantage of the law's lack of specificity to block efforts by the Agency to perform its coordination role. As a result, the Agency experienced its first of three near death experiences—barely surviving the turf wars that occurred during the Truman era. The key to its survival was the Agency's acceptance of responsibility for covert activities after both the new Defense Department and the State Department refused offers to take on this role. The CIA would go on to face two more near death experiences—at the end of the Cold War and in the wake of the attacks of September 11.

The third innovation of the 1947 National Security Act was the NME, which brought the Army, Navy, and newly established Air Force under a single department. Pearl Harbor had confirmed the need for permanent military preparedness, which required both a large and well-equipped standing army and new institutions to give military representatives an influential role at the top of the policy-making community. This was a fundamental break from the tradition of a peacetime militia that had been in place since the founding of the Republic. Many wartime military leaders welcomed this change and began to prepare for a more active role in the formulation of American foreign policy when World War II ended. One example of the military's efforts to prepare for these new responsibilities was Major General George Lincoln's acceptance of a demotion to colonel in 1947, so that he could join the West Point faculty and help educate the next generation of officers in such areas as political science and economics. This new approach would come to be described as "pol-mil."

The new NME was headed by a secretary of defense who was expected to encourage cooperation between the three armed services—but without any real authority. James Forrestal, who was chosen as the first secretary of defense, admitted that he would "probably need the ... attention ... of the entire psychiatric profession" by the end of his first year on the job.[15] Which begs the question why Forrestal would accept Truman's invitation to serve as the first secretary of defense, since no one knew better than Forrestal how frustratingly weak the new office was. The answer to this question can be found in the wording of the legislation, which designated the secretary of defense as the president's "principal assistant ... in all matters relating to the national security." This encouraged Forrestal to believe that the weakness of his position within the NME was not important since he would be serving in a more important capacity as the person who would oversee the entire new national security system whenever the president was not present. With this in mind, the secretary began to make plans for locating the entire NSC staff in the Pentagon, and drawing almost the entire NSC staff from the armed forces.[16] At the first meeting of the NSC, however, the president announced that the secretary of state would preside over Council meetings in his absence. Forrestal's efforts to be "first among equals" in the new national security bureaucracy were blocked, and the secretary was forced to concentrate his time and energy on the impossible task of seeking cooperation among the three independent armed services. It seems reasonable to describe this entire episode as Truman's revenge for Forrestal's opposition to the president's unification plan. Two years later, the NSA was amended to eliminate any future confusion, designating the secretary of defense as the "principal assistant to the President in all matters relating to the Department of Defense." Subsequent amendments to the 1947 Act—in 1953, 1958, and 1986—helped bolster the authority of the secretary within the Department of Defense, and to move the armed services closer to Truman's vision of "all the reins in one hand." For the most part, this has been a very positive trend, but as I will discuss later in this essay, it has contributed to the transformation of the Washington policy-making community from a pol-mil system to a "mil-pol" system.

One more agency created by the 1947 Act deserves mention at this point, because it was envisioned as being as important as the NSC. This was the National Security Resources Board (NSRB). Its duties were vaguely defined in the legislation, but it was assumed that it would be responsible for advising the president on economic issues that could affect the nation's ability to rapidly transition from peace to war. Once the agency was up and running, however, it attempted to play a much more ambitious role in the management of the nation's economy, addressing issues of stockpiling, civil defense, industrial production, and the location of factories to "better survive nuclear attack." Both Truman and Eisenhower opposed efforts by the NSRB to expand its authority, and by 1953, the agency had been disbanded. Truman and Eisenhower's opposition to the NSRB was consistent with the advice that Secretary of War Henry Stimson had given to FDR at the start of World War II—that even in wartime, a capitalist country had to "let business make money. ..."[17] From the point of view of institutional architecture, however, the disappearance of the NSRB left a hole in the national security bureaucracy—and every president since that time has had to establish ad hoc procedures for linking national security issues with economic considerations.

The other important agency that demands comment in any discussion of the creation of the national security bureaucracy is the State Department. After the shock of Pearl Harbor, State lost its advantageous position as the lead agency in the formulation of U.S. foreign policy. In the months prior to the passage of the NSA, Secretary of State George Marshall tried to convince Truman that the proposed NSC would be a threat to the president's constitutionally designated authority. He also warned that the military would dominate the NSC, making the secretary of state "the automaton of the Council."[18] The secretary also opposed the creation of the CIA, on the grounds that the collection and analysis of information relating to foreign affairs was the historically established role of the State Department. Although Truman was sympathetic to Marshall's concerns, he had decided by this time that he needed closure on the issue of institutional reform.

Faced with a choice between supporting the new system that would favor the national security institutions, or fighting a losing battle to preserve a national interest-based approach to foreign policy, the State Department leadership opted for the first option and attempted to demonstrate its indispensability to the new goal of preparedness. Under the leadership of Marshall and Dean Acheson, State was able to hold its own during the Truman era, by demonstrating its *bona fides* as a national security organization and by relying on the Policy Planning Staff to shape the initial debates about the nature and implications of the Soviet threat. But with the arrival of the Eisenhower administration, it became clear that the center of gravity had shifted to the NSC.

Eisenhower had made it clear during the presidential campaign that he intended to improve the efficiency of the NSC and rely upon it to make and manage foreign policy. His negative opinion of Truman's management of the NSC was shared by his secretary of state, John Foster Dulles, who blamed much of what he saw as confusion and competition within the Truman administration on the State Department and its secretary. Once he took over at Foggy Bottom, Dulles supported the president's decision to designate the special assistant to the president for national security affairs, rather than the secretary of state, as the person who would lead NSC deliberations when the president was absent.[19] In his first conversation as secretary of state with Paul

Nitze, the head of the State Department's Policy Planning Staff, Dulles made it clear that the relationship between State and NSC had turned a corner. Dulles commended the Policy Planning Staff for its work up to that time, but then informed Nitze that issues relating to national security would henceforth be "placed directly under the control of the National Security Council." He informed Nitze that he planned to "devote ninety-five percent of his own time" to national security issues and that he would leave the management of State to his deputy, Walter Bedell Smith.[20] From this point until the present, the State Department has been fighting a rear-guard campaign to preserve its status and influence within the Washington policy community.

One of the great ironies of the Cold War era was that a system created to insure against the next Pearl Harbor was, in fact, a pretty good fit for the demands of anti-Soviet containment. An intelligence community that performed both covert operations and information gathering and analysis, a massive American military force backed by a global network of alliances and armed with the "absolute weapon," and a decision-making system that was designed to identify and respond to threats to the national security all contributed to Washington's ultimate victory over Moscow. Of course, the politics of preparedness was not without costs, including an acceptance of budget deficits as a normal state of affairs and a difficulty differentiating between major threats and minor problems. Furthermore, the characteristic of the Pearl Harbor system that made it effective during the Cold War—the narrow focus on one over-riding military threat at the expense of other national priorities—made this approach to foreign policy entirely inappropriate for the post-Cold War era.

Some commentators did make the case for a new post-Cold War network of institutions capable of articulating and sustaining a multifaceted foreign policy consistent with the traditional concept of national interests. After all, the threat that had justified about eighty percent of U.S. spending on defense and intelligence was gone, and America found itself in what Richard Haass has described as an "uncommonly benign" environment that presented the United States with a unique opportunity to "adjust its foreign policy to cooperate more with other countries."[21] Unfortunately, the debate about institutional reform never gained traction, in part because there was no political benefit to be derived from questioning the value of the institutions that had been instrumental in winning the struggle against the Soviet Union. Washington therefore continued to view world affairs through the lens of national security and preparedness.

A decade after the fall of the Berlin Wall, General William Navas argued that the nation could not wait for the next "burning platform" to spur the debate for institutional reform.[22] One year later, on September 11, the nation had its burning platform. On the fifth anniversary of the attack, President Bush stated that "For America, 9/11 was more than a tragedy, it changed the way we look at the world."[23] On the contrary, 9/11 validated and reinforced a way of looking at the world that had been in place since 1941. "No more Pearl Harbors" had been the *sine qua non* of American foreign policy for six decades, and now our government had failed this test. This helps to explain what David Rothkopf has called the Bush administration's "disproportionate" response to 9/11: "rather than treating the attack as a manifestation of a new, different, and more limited type of threat, they [Bush administration] reflexively responded with the strategies of traditional warfare approaches that had once been reserved for states." Rothkopf goes on to speculate that "Perhaps we needed to enlarge the enemy to be commensurate with the damage done to our collective psyche."[24] Or, perhaps after serving the demands of preparedness for sixty years, America was bound to overreact when preparedness ultimately failed.

The shock of 9/11 had consequences not just for U.S. policies overseas but for the national security bureaucracy as well. Some significant institutional and procedural adjustments did occur following the 9/11 attacks, including the creation of the Department of Homeland Security and the Office of the Director of National Intelligence. But the window of opportunity for any debate about comprehensive reform of the U.S. policy-making machinery was slammed shut, and remains so today.

In the fifteen years that have elapsed since the 9/11 attacks, numerous experts and policy makers have identified serious problems in the way U.S. foreign policy is made and managed. Two common complaints bear special mention. The first complaint relates to the militarization of American foreign policy. There are three aspects to this issue, the first of which is commonly referred to as the 800-pound gorilla problem—the disproportionate influence of the military in the policy-making process. Professor Eliot Cohen has argued that we have nothing to fear as long as our military leaders continue to accept the fact that they are engaged in an "unequal dialogue" with their civilian superiors.[25] The problem is, however, that there are actually two unequal dialogues at work here. On the one hand, our military leaders do not question the principle of subordination to their constitutionally designated civilian masters, but on the other hand, military representatives are so much more influential than their civilian counterparts in the day-to-day formulation of U.S. foreign policy that it is difficult for Washington to interpret and respond to events in ways that are not militarized. The fact that the 800-pound gorilla problem is attributable in large part to the military's record of reliable service and the efforts that the armed services have made to train and educate their leaders does not make the situation any less serious.

This leads directly to the second aspect of the problem—the so-called hammer-and-nail issue—defined as the over-reliance on the armed forces to manage problems that should be handled by civilian agencies. The Obama administration's pivot to the Indo-Asia-Pacific region nicely illustrates this issue. Although the rhetoric relating to the U.S. pivot stresses the need for a multifaceted campaign of political, economic, and military engagement, the fact is that the president's advisers had no alternative but to construct the pivot campaign around the so-called San Francisco system of alliances and security relationships across the Indo-Asia-Pacific region. We had to play to our strengths in order to offset China's economic and geopolitical advantages. In doing so, however, we have made it easier for Beijing to depict the United States as a one-trick pony, whose emphasis on military policies is inconsistent with, or actually threatening to, the diplomatic and economic priorities of many nations in the region.[26]

The military's dominance of the policy-making process and the over-reliance on the armed services for policy implementation would be less of a problem if there was an atmosphere of trust and familiarity between civilian and military policy makers. Americans can take great pride in their nation's history of military subordination to civilian authority, but four decades after the creation of the All-Volunteer Force, the American military has taken on many of the characteristics of a military class that is relatively isolated from the U.S. population that it is sworn to serve. Former Secretary of Defense Robert Gates communicated his concern about this third trend in civil-military relations when he warned the cadets at West Point about a situation that "risks fostering a closed culture of superiority and aloofness."[27]

So, what is to be done? Many commentators and policy makers have called for reforms that will rebalance the playing field between the military and civilian policy-making communities. Some of these individuals have made the case for a "Goldwater-Nichols for the interagency" or a "whole of government" arrangement that would make it easier for various civilian agencies to gain a seat at the table as circumstances required. The Obama administration attempted to address this problem by enlarging NSC membership to about 400 people. Derek Chollet has noted that "this is less a power grab and more a reflection of global complexity and a changing world."[28] Inevitably, however, any attempt to make the NSC look more like a plateau than a "policy hill" must confront problems of time and resource management. The White House recently admitted as much when it announced that it was "reversing the trend of growth" in order to make the NSC staff more "lean, nimble, and policy oriented."[29]

Some commentators have also looked beyond the NSC to enhance civilian capacity in Washington, citing the State Department as the logical counterweight to the armed services and calling for its reestablishment as the lead agency in the foreign policy community. It is at least possible that President Hillary Clinton will make this case, since she will be the first former Secretary of State to become president since James Buchanan. During her tenure as secretary of state, Clinton took steps to enhance the status and influence of her agency, the most notable of which was the launch of the Quadrennial Diplomacy and Development Review (QDDR) in 2010. The QDDR was a modest first step toward getting the State Department back into the policy formulation game that has been dominated by the military for decades. But any attempt to go further would run up against the entrenched prejudices against the State Department that are shared by Congress and the American people. During the just-completed presidential campaign, candidate Clinton was well aware that there was no benefit in making a strong argument for bolstering the State Department. Of the 32 issues that she listed on her official campaign website, there was no mention of the need to strengthen State.

The second argument that is often heard regarding the national security bureaucracy is the need for new mechanisms and procedures for formulating and sustaining strategy. American foreign policy since the end of the Cold War has often seemed to validate Robert McNamara's claim that "there is no longer such a thing as strategy, there is only crisis management."[30] It is not that we lack strategy documents. Indeed, we have far too many documents that send far too many disparate signals in the service of incompatible interests and goals. Small wonder, then, that even the *National Security Strategy*, the document that is supposed to serve as the north star for an administration's foreign policy, is often viewed in Washington and around the world as an "aspirational document"—just another wish list that does not have to be taken very seriously. What is needed is an influential institutional actor capable of assisting in the development of an administration's strategy and then, more importantly, serving as the defender and promoter of that strategy in day-to-day policy debates.

The first logical candidate for this role is the Policy Planning Staff at State, which was established by Secretary of State George Marshall to perform precisely this type of strategy formulation function. Reestablishing the Policy Planning Staff as the lead agency for strategic planning has merit, since it would help address both of the problems that have been discussed—it would help to "civilianize" the policy-making process, while at the same time assisting in strategy articulation and implementation. But moving in this direction would require a major overhaul of a Policy Planning Staff, which has acquired numerous administrative responsibilities (special projects, organizing meetings, speech writing, etc.) over the years.[31] More importantly, any attempt to give the State Department a leadership role in strategic planning would run into the same problems of lack of public trust and support mentioned earlier.

Another institutional player that is occasionally cited as a candidate for the articulation and sustainment of strategy is the Office of the Vice President. This idea is attractive because it would establish a clear role for an office that has been growing in size and responsibility since the Clinton era. According to the official Senate website, the Office of the Vice President is the "least understood, most ridiculed, and most often ignored office in the Federal Government."[32] But, in fact, it has become a valuable utility infielder for three administrations, particularly on issues relating to foreign affairs and national security. It is understandable under these circumstances that some experts would see this office as a candidate for the role of shepherd of the president's strategy. There are, however, two characteristics of the vice presidency that raise doubts about this person's reliability as the president's institutionalized agent. First, most vice presidents view the office as a path to the presidency. Second, the president cannot fire his VP. Neither of these characteristics is conducive to a high level of trust on the part of the president.

Since neither the State Department nor the Office of Vice President is likely to be given responsibility for the formulation and sustainment of strategy, a strategic planning cell within the NSC seems like the best option. There have been several attempts to develop such a strategic planning cell within the NSC, but these initiatives have tended to be understaffed and overwhelmed by events. David Rothkopf describes the atmosphere within the NSC as "constant, frenzied reaction." He goes on to assert that "Planning seems not only a luxury, but almost a dereliction of duty given the pressures of the moment."[33] If adequately staffed and resourced, however, and if it is given sufficient support by the president, there is no reason why such a strategy cell could not be fenced off from the day-to-day churn of the NSC so that it could focus on the formulation and sustainment of the president's strategic priorities. If such a cell is to avoid the aforementioned problems of militarization, however, it will have to be composed of representatives of the civilian foreign policy agencies who have the clout and experience needed to balance the influence of well-trained and well-staffed members of the armed services.

The U.S. pivot to the Indo-Asia-Pacific would be a good test for any new agency responsible for articulating and sustaining U.S. strategy, since the pivot will have to continue as the nation's top strategic priority for the foreseeable future. Responding to the shift in the global base of gravity from West to East will not be an option for the next administration; it will be an essential adjustment to geostrategic and geoeconomic realities. President Obama is to be commended for recognizing this fact, but in the absence of an agency dedicated to the sustainment of his strategy, it has been difficult for the Obama administration to avoid being overwhelmed by the inbox.

Conclusion

The shock of Pearl Harbor led to the creation of a network of national security institutions designed around two questions: Where is the threat? and Who is the enemy? This Pearl Harbor system served its purpose during the Cold War, but since that time the costs associated with this narrow and reactive approach to foreign policy formulation have outweighed the benefits. In an essay written in 1952, Arnold Wolfers asserted that "Security is a value ... of which a nation can have more or less. ... [E]very increment of security must be paid for by additional sacrifices of other values. ... At a certain point, by something like the economic law of diminishing returns, the gain in security no longer compensates for the added costs of attaining it."[34] One of the most severe costs that we have incurred has been a gradual erosion of our ability to articulate, debate, and manage policies based on a multifaceted conception of the national interest.

It would be naive and misleading to conclude with a claim that we have nothing to fear but fear itself. America faces a wide range of traditional and nontraditional threats that will continue to demand efficient national security planning. But seventy-five years after the Pearl Harbor attack, it is time to place national security back in the context of a foreign policy based on national interests, so that military issues can be systematically and explicitly weighed against competing economic, political, and diplomatic priorities. In the conclusion to their new book, *War By Other Means*, Robert Blackwill and Jennifer Harris argue that in a situation in which America "faces a blizzard of international problems...perhaps it is best to return to a compelling compass for U.S. external behavior—American national interests as a basis for U.S. grand strategy."[35]

There is no way to accomplish this fundamental change that does not involve a significant enhancement of the State Department's status and influence in Washington and around the world. In his contribution to this volume, James Steinberg provides an excellent start to discussions about strengthening State. Readers will note that his title is a nod to Dean Acheson's book—*Present at the Creation*. This book is still the gold standard for political memoirs, in part because of Acheson's wonderfully cynical sense of humor. One example is his account of the celebration held in Washington on the occasion of the signing of the NATO treaty. Acheson commends the Marine Corps band for their "unexpected realism" in choosing to play "I Got Plenty of Nothin" and "It Ain't Necessarily So" during the festivities.[36] Acheson's book deserves mention both because it discusses many of the challenges that the State Department continues to face, but more importantly because the author is often the harshest critic of his own agency—citing its reticence to grasp opportunities for advancement in the scrum of bureaucratic politics. Acheson leveled some of his most withering criticism at his colleagues in Foggy Bottom who rejected Truman's offer to make State the lead agency in intelligence analysis. Depending on how things played out, this one institutional reform might have permanently established State as the gatekeeper between the president and the other foreign policy agencies. The themes of missed opportunities and self-inflicted wounds that permeate Acheson's memoir are also present in the State Department's first QDDR in 2010—which reads at some points like an institutional *mea culpa*.[37]

At one level, at least, the need for a State Department-led, national interests approach to U.S. foreign policy would seem to be a relatively easy argument to make, since it is compatible with the kinds of policies that have been recommended by most of America's influential experts on world affairs, including Richard Haass's call for a foreign policy of "integration," Joseph Nye's arguments in support of "smart power strategies," Zbigniew Brzezinski's call for "renovation" and "revitalization," Fareed Zakaria's call for American adjustment to the "rise of the rest," and Henry Kissinger's call for a "strategy and diplomacy that allow for the complexity of the journey."[38] Unfortunately, these experts write as strategists, for an audience of strategists. Implicit in this type of argument is the assumption that fundamental reform of the national security bureaucracy is a policy choice among elites. In fact, the problem is much deeper and will require a gradual adjustment in the way that Americans think about foreign affairs. Preparedness is the lens through which Americans look at the world and define situations. This will not change easily, as illustrated by the criticisms that President Obama has faced when he has attempted to tamp down alarmist rhetoric relating to incidents at home or crises abroad.[39]

In the end, any campaign to reestablish State as the lead agency in the foreign-policy-making system will require the sustained support of what Harold Koh has called a "strong plebiscitary president."[40] Until we have a president who is willing and able to invest the political capital in the service of fundamental institutional reform, we are best served by small steps designed to cope with the most problematic aspects of the Pearl Harbor system. The cooperation between former Secretary of

Defense Gates and former Secretary of State Clinton in support of enhanced civilian capacity is a good example of an informal improvement. Anne-Marie Slaughter's recommendation that when the NSC initiates a project, it should designate a lead agency to manage that project is a simple procedural adjustment that could significantly enhance the influence of agencies such as the State Department.[41] Also deserving of mention is a very valuable initiative sponsored by the Andrew Mellon Foundation to help close the civilian-military "gap." Over the last six years, funds provided by the Mellon Foundation have allowed thousands of students from seven liberal arts colleges and seven military education institutions to come together in academic and social contexts in order to become more familiar with, and more trusting of, each other.

This volume provides many other recommendations for reform of the national security bureaucracy that deserve to be considered by the incoming president.

Douglas Stuart is the first holder of the Stuart Chair in International Studies at Dickinson College. He is also an adjunct research professor at the U.S. Army War College. Professor Stuart has published over thirty articles, five monographs, and ten books, including *Creating the National Security State* (Princeton, 2008) and *Organizing for National Security* (U.S. Army War College, 2000). His research interests include the history of the U.S. national security bureaucracy, civil-military relations, and the American "pivot" to the Indo-Asia-Pacific region. His most recent publication is *The Pivot to Asia: Can it Serve as the Foundation for American Grand Strategy in the 21st Century?* (Strategic Studies Monograph, U.S. Army War College, 2016). Professor Stuart is the director of the Mellon Foundation Project on Civilian-Military Educational Cooperation, which creates opportunities for academic and social interaction between students and faculty at selected liberal arts colleges and selected military education institutions in order to cultivate trust and familiarity between the two communities.

[1] See Neustadt, Richard, and Ernest May. 1986. *Thinking in Time: The Uses of History for Decision Makers.* New York: Free Press, 247-270.

[2] Portions of this essay draw upon arguments that are developed by Stuart, Douglas. 2008. *Creating the National Security State: A History of the Law that Transformed America.* Princeton, NJ: Princeton University Press and Stuart, Douglas. December 2008. "Constructing the Iron Cage: The 1947 National Security Act." In *Affairs of State: The Interagency and National Security*, edited by Gabriel Marcella, 53-96. Carlisle, PA: U.S. Army War College, Strategic Studies Institute.

[3] Ambrose, Stephen, and Douglas Brinkley. 2010. *Rise to Globalism*, 9th edition. New York: Penguin. Regarding the priority that the State Department accorded to geoeconomics in the nineteenth century, see Blackwill, Robert, and Jennifer Harris. 2016. *War By Other Mean: Geoeconomics and Statecraft.* Cambridge, MA: Harvard University Press, 154-157.

[4] May, Ernest. 1988. "The Development of Political-Military Consultation in the United States." Reprinted in *Decisions of the Highest Order: Perspectives on the National Security Council*, edited by Karl Inderfurth and Loch Johnson, 9. Belmont, CA: Brooks/Cole Publishing.

[5] See, for example, Beard, Charles. 1934. *The Idea of National Interest*. New York: MacMillan.

[6] Quoted by Brinkley, David. 1988. *Washington Goes to War*. New York: Knopf, 27.

[7] See the author's discussion of national interests in Stuart, Douglas. 2008. *Creating the National Security State*. Princeton, NJ: Princeton University Press, 22-28.

[8] de Seversky, Alexander. 1942. *Victory Through Air Power*. New York: Simon and Schuster, 18-19.

[9] Hobbes, Thomas. 1974. *Leviathan*. Edited by Michael Oakeshott, 101. New York: Collier MacMillan.

[10] Truman, Harry. August 26, 1944. "Our Armed Forces Must be Unified." *Collier's*, quoted in Stuart, Douglas. 2008. *Creating the National Security State: A History of the Law that Transformed America*. Princeton, NJ: Princeton University Press, 86.

[11] Quoted by Stuart, Douglas. 2013. "Preparing for the Next Pearl Harbor: Harry Truman's Role in the Creation of the U.S. National Security Establishment." In *Origins of the National Security State and the Legacy of Harry S. Truman*, edited by Mary Ann Heiss and Michael Hogan, 18. Kirksville, MO: Truman State University Press.

[12] Norstad discussion with Forrestal, James. 1951. *The Forrestal Diaries*, edited by Walter Millis. New York: Viking Press, 315.

[13] See the author's analysis in Stuart, Douglas. 2013. "Preparing for the Next Pearl Harbor: Harry Truman's Role in the Creation of the U.S. National Security Establishment." In *Origins of the National Security State and the Legacy of Harry S. Truman*, edited by Mary Ann Heiss and Michael Hogan, 26-27. Kirksville, MO: Truman State University Press.

[14] See Ranelagh, John. 1986. *The Agency: The Rise and Decline of the CIA, From Wild Bill Donovan to William Casey*. New York: Simon and Schuster, 110.

[15] Quoted in Forrestal, James. 1951. *The Forrestal Diaries*, edited by Walter Millis. New York: Viking Press, 300.

[16] Clifford, Clark, and Richard Holbrook. 1991. *Counsel to the President*. New York: Random House, 162-163.

[17] Quoted by Gropman, Alan. 1996. *Mobilizing U.S. Industry for World War II: Myth and Reality*, McNair Paper #50. Washington, DC: National Defense University, 5.

[18] Quoted in Stuart, Douglas. 2008. *Creating the National Security State: A History of the Law that Transformed America*. Princeton, NJ: Princeton University Press, 129.

[19] See Bowie, Robert, and Richard Immerman. 1998. *Waging Peace: How Eisenhower Shaped an Enduring Cold War Strategy*. New York: Oxford University Press, 85-90.

[20] Nitze, Paul. 1989. *From Hiroshima to Glasnost: At the Center of Decision*. New York: Grove Wedenfield, 142.

[21] Haass, Richard. 2005. *The Opportunity*. New York: Public Affairs, 197-198. The closest that our nation came to taking advantage of this opportunity was the Clinton administration's argument in support of an enlargement and engagement strategy. Unfortunately, this effort was ultimately overwhelmed by successive crises.

[22] November 2000. "The National Security Act of 2002." In *Organizing for National Security*, edited by Douglas Stuart, 240. Carlisle, PA: U.S. Army War College, Strategic Studies Institute.

[23] September 11, 2006. "President Bush's Address to the Nation." *New York Times.*

[24] Rothkopf, David. 2014. *National Insecurity: American Leadership in an Age of Fear.* New York: Public Affairs, 30 and 32.

[25] Cohen, Eliot A. 2002. *Supreme Command: Soldiers, Statesmen, and Leadership in Wartime.* New York: Free Press, 208-224.

[26] See the analysis of Obama's policies in Stuart, Douglas. August 2016. *The Pivot to Asia: Can it Serve as the Foundation for American Grand Strategy in the 21st Century?* Carlisle, PA: U.S. Army War College, Strategic Studies Institute. http://www.strategicstudiesinstitute.army.mil/pubs/display.cfm?pubID=1326

[27] Gates, Robert. October 6, 2011. "Robert M. Gates Thayer Award Remarks," at U.S. Military Academy, West Point, NY. http://www.westpointaog.org/page.aspx?pid=4843

[28] Chollet, Derek. April 26, 2016. "What's Wrong with Obama's National Security Council?" *Defense One.* http://www.defenseone.com/ideas/2016/04/whats-wrong-obamas-national-security-council/127802/

[29] Goldfien, Michael. March 30, 2016. "How the NSC Hijacked U.S. Foreign Policy." *The National Interest.* http://nationalinterest.org/feature/how-the-nsc-hijacked-us-foreign-policy-15625

[30] McNamara testimony before congress, quoted in Bell, Coral. 1971. *The Conventions of Crisis.* London: Oxford University Press, 2.

[31] See the description of the Policy Planning Staff's duties on the official State Department website, http://www.state.gov/s/p/.

[32] http://www.senate.gov/artandhistory/history/common/briefing/Vice_President.htm. See also, Gaudion, Amy, and Douglas Stuart. July 19, 2012. "More than Just a Running Mate." *The New York Times.* http://campaignstops.blogs.nytimes.com/2012/07/19/more-than-just-a-running-mate/?_r=0

[33] Rothkopf, David. 2004. *Running the World: The Inside Story of the National Security Council and the Architects of American Power.* New York: Public Affairs, 459.

[34] Wolfers, Arnold. 1962. "National Security as an Ambiguous Symbol." Reprinted in *Discord and Collaboration: Essays on International Politics.* Baltimore: Johns Hopkins Press, 150 and 158.

[35] Blackwill, Robert D., and Jennifer M. Harris. *War By Other Means: Geoeconomics and Statecraft.* Cambridge, MA: Harvard University Press, 254.

[36] Acheson, Dean. 1969. *Present at the Creation: My Years in the State Department.* New York: WW Norton, 284.

[37] For a survey of some of the problems faced by the State Department, see Schake, Kori. 2012. *State of Disrepair: Fixing the Culture and Practices of the State Department.* Stanford, CA: Hoover Institution Press.

[38] Haass, Richard. 2005. *The Opportunity.* New York: Public Affairs, 24-25; Nye, Joseph. 2011. *The Future of Power.* New York: Public Affairs, 207-234; Brzezinski, Zbigniew. 2012. *Strategic Vision.* New York: Basic Books, 184-185; Zakaria, Fareed. 2008. *The Post-American World.* New York: Norton, 1-6; and Kissinger, Henry. 2014. *World Order.* New York: Penguin, 372.

[39] In Friedman, Uri. August 15, 2016. "Learning to Live with Terrorism." *The Atlantic,* the author discusses the criticisms that have been levelled against Obama for his assertions that "Jihadist terrorism is a manageable threat. ..." http://www.theatlantic.com/international/archive/2016/08/terrorism-resilience-isis/493433/

[40] Koh, Harold. 1990. *The National Security Constitution: Sharing Power After the Iran-Contra Affair.* New Haven, CT: Yale University Press, 102.

[41] Slaughter, Anne-Marie. 2016. "A Lead Agency for Every Security Initiative." *Democracy Journal* 39 (Winter). http://democracyjournal.org/magazine/39/a-lead-agency-for-every-security-initiative/

"Reflecting on a wide range of administrations, we have come to realize the crucial importance in American foreign policy making of the history deficit: the fact that key decision-makers know alarmingly little not just of other countries' pasts, but also of their own."

—GRAHAM ALLISON AND NIALL FERGUSON

Establish a White House Council of Historical Advisers Now

Graham Allison
Director
Belfer Center for Science and International Affairs
Harvard University

Niall Ferguson
Senior Fellow
Hoover Institution
Stanford University

Applied history is the explicit attempt to illuminate current challenges and choices by analyzing historical precedents and analogues. Mainstream historians begin with a past event or era and attempt to provide an account of what happened and why. Applied historians begin with a current choice or predicament and attempt to analyze the historical record to provide perspective, stimulate imagination, find clues about what is likely to happen, suggest possible policy interventions, and assess probable consequences. It might be said that applied history is to mainstream history as medical practice is to biochemistry, or engineering to physics. But that analogy is not quite right, as in the realm of science there is mutual respect between practitioners and theorists. In the realm of policy, by contrast, one finds a culture of mutual contempt between practitioners and historians. Applied history is an attempt to address that.

The Applied History Project at Harvard's Kennedy School seeks to revitalize the study and practice of history in the tradition of two twentieth century giants: the modern historian Ernest May and the leading analyst of the American presidency, Richard Neustadt. Their book *Thinking in Time*, published in 1986, provides the foundation on which we intend to build.[1] An urgently needed companion volume might be titled *Acting in Time*. Over the past decade, particularly as one of us was engaged in research for a biography of Henry Kissinger, we shared a humbling epiphany. It has been said that most Americans live in the "United States of Amnesia." What we had not fully appreciated is how often this includes American policy makers as well. Reflecting on a wide range of administrations, we have come to realize the crucial importance in American foreign policy making of the *history deficit*: the fact that key decision-makers know alarmingly little not just of other countries' pasts, but also of their own.

Speaking about his book, *Doomed to Succeed: The U.S.-Israel Relationship from Truman to Obama*, veteran U.S. diplomat Dennis Ross recently noted that "almost no administration's leading figures know the history of what we have done in the Middle East."[2] Neither do they know the history of the region itself. In 2003, when President George Bush chose to topple Saddam Hussein and replace his regime with an elected government that represented the majority of Iraqis, he did not appear to appreciate either the difference between Sunni and Shiite Muslims or the significance of the fact that Saddam's regime was led by a Sunni minority that had suppressed the Shiite majority. He failed to heed warnings that the predictable consequence of this choice would be a Shiite-dominated Baghdad beholden to the Shiite champion in the Middle East—Iran. Indeed, in attempting to explain the consequences of this fateful choice, one of the leaders from the region is reported to have told President Bush that if he cut down the tallest tree in the region (Saddam), he should not be surprised when he found the second tallest tree towering over the others.

The problem is by no means limited to the Middle East or to Bush. The Obama administration's inability or unwillingness to recognize the deep historical relationship between Russia and Ukraine left it blind to the predictable consequences of European Union initiatives in late 2013 and early 2014 to lead Ukraine down a path to membership in the EU and, in time, NATO. "I don't really even need George Kennan right now," Obama told the editor of the *New Yorker* in an interview published in January 2014, referring to one of the great applied historians of the early Cold War. Within two months Russia had annexed Crimea.

Even more remarkable, however, is the apparent ignorance of the Republican candidate for the presidency of the historical significance of his own foreign policy mantra, "America First."

While this history deficit is only one of the weaknesses in the foreign policy of recent administrations of both parties, it is one that is more amenable to repair than most. Yet to address this deficit it is not enough for a president occasionally to invite friendly historians to dinner, as Obama has been known to do. Nor is it enough to appoint a court historian, as John F. Kennedy did with Arthur M. Schlesinger Jr.

We urge the candidates currently running for president to announce now that, if elected, they will **establish a White House Council of Historical Advisers** analogous to the Council of Economic Advisers established after World War II. Several eminent historians made similar recommendations to Presidents Carter and Reagan during their administrations: the checkered record of U.S. foreign policy since 1977 suggests that, in failing to do so, Carter and Reagan missed a great opportunity. We suggest this council's charter begin with Thucydides' observation that "events of future history will be of the same nature—or nearly so—as the history of the past, so long as men are men." While applied historians will never be clairvoyants with an unclouded crystal ball, we agree with Winston Churchill that "the longer you can look back, the farther you can look forward." The next president's charge to this council should be to provide historical perspectives on contemporary problems.

Imagine that President Obama had such a council today. What assignments could he give them? How could their responses help inform choices he now faces?

Start with the most intractable issue the president and his national security team have been debating recently: What to do about ISIS? He could ask his applied historians whether or not we have even seen anything like this before, and if so, which precedents seem most similar? He could ask further what happened in those cases, and thus, what clues they offer about what might happen in this one. We infer from recent statements that the administration tends to see ISIS as essentially a new version of al-Qaeda, and the goal of policy is to decapitate it, as al-Qaeda was decapitated with the assassination of Osama bin Laden in 2011. But there is good reason to believe that ISIS is quite different in structure from al-Qaeda and may in fact be a classic acephalous network.

Our initial search for precedents and analogues for ISIS includes 50 prior cases of similarly brutal, fanatical, purpose-driven groups, including the Bolsheviks of the Russian Revolution. Deciding which characteristics of ISIS we consider most salient—for example, its revolutionary politics or its religious millenarianism—helps us to narrow this list to the most instructive analogues. A systematic study of these other cases could help steer the president away from a potentially erroneous equation of ISIS with its most recent forerunner.

That this kind of approach can be invaluable is illustrated by the U.S. government's response to the Great Recession of 2008. That September saw the biggest shock to the U.S. economy since the Great Depression. In 24 hours, the Dow Jones industrial average plummeted, credit swaps among major banks froze, and the shock spread almost instantly to international markets. In the words of then-Secretary of the Treasury Hank Paulson, "the 'system-wide' crisis was more severe and unpredictable than any in our lifetimes." For that reason, historical knowledge of earlier financial crises—and particularly the Great Depression that began in 1929—was at a premium.

It was sheer good luck that the chairman of the Federal Reserve from 2006 to 2014 was also a serious student of economic history. As Ben Bernanke wrote in his 2015 memoir, "understanding what was happening in the context of history proved invaluable" because "the crisis of 2007-2009 was best understood as a descendant of the classic financial panics of the nineteenth and early twentieth centuries."[3] The specter that haunted Bernanke most was the Great Depression of 1929. While some criticized his "obsession" with the post-1929 depression, there can be no doubt about his commitment not to repeat the mistakes that contributed to that catastrophe.

In a 2010 speech, Bernanke identified lessons from the Great Depression for policy makers today: "First, economic prosperity depends on financial stability; second, policy makers must respond forcefully, creatively, and decisively to severe financial crises; third, crises that are international in scope require an international response." Bernanke's Fed acted decisively, inventing unprecedented initiatives that stretched—if not exceeded—the Fed's legal powers, such as purchasing not only bonds issued by the federal government but also mortgage-backed and other securities in what was called "quantitative easing." The speed of the Fed's international initiatives to backstop other central banks and persuade them to collaborate in cutting short-term interest rates so as to enhance stability can also be traced back to Bernanke's knowledge of mistakes made in the Great Depression. Although the recent crisis took place in a radically different financial and economic context, Bernanke wrote in the conclusion of his memoir, "it rhymed with past panics."

Just as the financial storm was gathering, our colleagues Carmen Reinhart and Ken Rogoff were just completing a decade of research during which they had assembled a database of 350 financial crises over the past eight centuries. Their book *This Time is Different: Eight Centuries of Financial Folly* explicitly analyzed "precedents and analogues" with a view to illuminating current events. In testimony to Congress and a series of op-eds in late 2008 and early 2009, they argued that recessions caused by financial crises tend to persist for much longer than business-cycle recessions. Indeed, they opined that the "current crisis could mean stunted U.S. growth for at least five to seven more years," and that it would leave behind a legacy of significantly higher public debt.[4] Though hotly contested at the time by those who claimed that monetary and fiscal stimulus would achieve a rapid "v-shaped" recovery, their historically derived insights have proven prescient.

While Western economies stagnated, China continued its meteoric growth and increasingly realized its ability to reap geopolitical benefits from its newfound financial power. Will China's rise result in war with the United States? In a chapter written for the 2009 volume *Power and Restraint*, Ernest May offered an instructive demonstration of how the analysis of analogues and precedents can provide clues about "alternative patterns that might play out in U.S.-Chinese relationships." To do this, he considered "experience at the turn of the century and in the 1920s that can be instructive in suggesting some of the processes that engendered enmity or friendship across national boundaries." Specifically, he compared and contrasted interactions between Britain and two rising powers: Germany on the one hand, and the United States on the other. Britain and Germany, he notes, could have remained at peace since they "were essentially similar in culture, values, and institutions." "Why," then, "did the next two decades see Britain and Germany instead become enemies?" "Why did Britain not react to America's challenges as to those from Germany?"

May's analysis is subtle and nuanced, as it always was. In the first case, he concluded that "most of the blame has to go to Germany and its willful ruler, Kaiser Wilhelm II." Indeed, he argued that "the central reason for Germany's self-destructive behavior was that the kaiser and his ministers were preoccupied with their own domestic politics." "Wilhelm and his ministers found it useful—almost necessary—to have trouble abroad in order to maintain quiet at home." Reflecting on the consequences, he drew a telling lesson for China: "the example of Imperial Germany clearly warns how dangerous it can be for a rising power to use foreign policy as a means of satisfying domestic political needs."

In contrast, by finding ways to accommodate a rising United States, Britain demonstrated "how a great nation can benefit from swallowing its pride and being guided by long-term calculations of interest, both international and domestic." In the shaping of British foreign policy, "a chain of British decision-makers calculated coldly that the cost of resisting American pretentions would be too high." May thus applauded the British government's wise choice "to make a virtue of necessity and to yield to the Americans in every dispute with as good grace as was permitted." When a Liberal government came to power in 1906, British policy culminated in the new Foreign Secretary's declaration that "the pursuit and maintenance of American friendship was and would be a 'cardinal policy' of the United Kingdom."

As one of us has argued, another analogy for the U.S.-China relationship can be found as early as the tensions between ancient Athens and Sparta. As the Athenian historian Thucydides explained brilliantly in his account of the Peloponnesian War,

"What made war inevitable was the growth of Athenian power and the fear which this caused in Sparta." The Thucydides Trap—the inevitable structural stress that occurs when a rapidly rising power threatens to displace a ruling power—serves as the best framework available for thinking about U.S.-China relations today and in the years ahead. One of us has led a team of researchers at Harvard Kennedy School's Belfer Center that reviewed the leading historical accounts of the last 500 years and identified 16 cases when this occurred. In 12 of those cases, the outcome was war. The study represents one possible answer a Council of Historical Advisers could give to the president if he asked whether or not precedents exist for the current U.S.-China relationship.

To be sure, as Ernest May repeatedly reminded students and policy makers alike, historical analogies are easy to get wrong. Amateur analogies were commonplace in the wake of the 9/11 attacks, ranging from the then-president's own comparison with Pearl Harbor to the even worse parallels drawn by some members of his administration between Saddam Hussein and the leaders of the World War II Axis powers. To guard against such errors, May counseled that when considering a historical analogy, one should always follow a simple procedure: put the analogy as the headline on a sheet of paper; draw a straight line down the middle of the page; write "similar" at the top of one column and "different" at the top of the other; and then set to work. If you are unable to list at least three points of similarity and three of difference, then you should consult a historian.

To apply this "May Method" amid the flurry of analogizing on the 100th anniversary of the outbreak of World War I, one of us compared challenges facing U.S. and Chinese leaders today with those faced by European leaders in 1914.[5] That analysis highlighted seven salient similarities as well as seven instructive differences, and concluded that "the probability of war between the United States and China in the decade ahead is higher than I imagined before examining the analogy—but still unlikely. Indeed, if statesmen in both countries reflect on what happened a century ago, perspective and insights from this past can be applied now to make risks of war even lower."

As the most consequential modern practitioner of applied history, Henry Kissinger, put it, "History is not a cookbook offering pretested recipes. It teaches by analogy, not by maxims." History "illuminates the consequences of actions in comparable situations." But—and here is the art that requires both imagination and judgment—for it to do so, "each generation must discover for itself what situations are in fact comparable."

"Is it unprecedented?" is just one of a number of questions or assignments that we propose the president could give his or her Council of Historical Advisers. Others include:

- What lessons of statecraft from a former president's handling of another crisis could be applied to a current challenge? (What would X have done?)
- What is the significance of a historical anniversary for the present (a common topic for presidential speeches)?
- What is the relevant history of the state, institution, or issue at hand?
- What if some action had not been taken (the kind of question too seldom asked after a policy failure)?
- Grand strategic questions like "Can the United States avoid decline?"
- Speculative questions about seemingly improbable future scenarios.

Most presidents have a favorite predecessor. In developing his strategy for meeting Iran's nuclear challenge, President Obama is reported to have reflected on WWKD? (What would Kennedy do?) His choice of an "ugly deal" to stop the advance of Iran's nuclear program rather than the bombing of its uranium enrichment plants (as Israeli Prime Minister Benjamin Netanyahu hoped he might) or acquiescing in an Iranian *fait accompli* (as some of his advisers thought inevitable) had some parallels with Kennedy's choices in the Cuban Missile Crisis to strike a deal with Nikita Khrushchev rather than risk an invasion of Cuba or learn to live with Soviet missiles off the Florida coast. Two key points were that the successful deal in 1962 was based on secret negotiations with Moscow—even though that unsettled some American allies—and that there was a middle ground between complete capitulation and nuclear war.

A third type of assignment the president could give his historians would be to take the anniversary of a major historical event as an occasion to reflect on current challenges. The ongoing centennial of World War I has provided leaders with an important opportunity to speak about its significance. Despite the fact that a general European war seemed to many contemporaries unthinkable, and despite the fact that the economies of Britain and Germany were so heavily interdependent, war broke out and proved impossible to end by diplomatic means. When it ended four years later with the disintegration of the Central Powers, more than ten million men had lost their lives prematurely, and Europe had been severely weakened.

In the decade before this war, the major governments had made a series of commitments to each other that created what Kissinger has called a "diplomatic doomsday machine." As the strategic competition between the United States and China in the South and East China Seas intensifies, applied historians could usefully carry out a serious review of U.S. commitments to Japan, the Philippines, and others that might one day function as a modern-day equivalent.

A fourth type of assignment suitable for the president's historians would be to determine the relevant history of the state, institution, or issue at hand, and how foreign counterparts understand that history. In dealing with foreign nations, we should never forget Henry Kissinger's observation that "history is the memory of states" and that "for nations, history plays the role that character confers on human beings." Learning the history of other nations, and honing the skills of historical enquiry in general, can help to promote cultural empathy. As Sir Michael Howard argued thirty-five years ago, any proper historical education must teach its students "how to step outside their own cultural skins and enter the minds of others; the minds not only of our own forebears, enormously valuable though this is, but of those of our contemporaries who have inherited a different experience from the past." Unfortunately, many of our elites can be, as Sir Michael put it, "people often of masterful intelligence, trained usually in law or economics or perhaps in political science, who have led their governments into disastrous decisions and miscalculations because they have no awareness whatsoever of the historical background, the cultural universe, of the foreign societies with which they have to deal." We cannot understand the decisions of key players in foreign nations without grasping how they themselves understand their nation's history, for, in Sir Michael's words, "all we believe about the present depends on what we believe about the past."

Therefore, in preparing to engage China's leaders, what might the next president ask his or her council? A useful starting assignment would be: How does Xi Jinping understand the arc of Chinese history and his role in China's future? Does he see his mission simply as rounding out China's economic development and restoring it to its historically "normal" role as the biggest country in the world after its "century of humiliation?" If so, we could expect to see the emergence of a richer and more confident China, but probably embedded in a "status quo" system still fundamentally shaped by U.S. power and institutions. Or does he also seek to revise the international order by displacing the United States as the predominant Asian and perhaps global power in the foreseeable future? In answering this assignment, the applied historians could draw on the recorded wisdom of a man who perhaps understood the worldview and historical consciousness of China's leaders better than anyone: the late leader of Singapore, Lee Kuan Yew. Lee—whom every Chinese leader since Deng Xiaoping, including Xi, has called a "mentor"—argued that "the size of China's displacement of the world balance is such that the world must find a new balance," and that China "wants to be China and accepted as such—not as an honorary member of the West." When asked if China's leaders wish to supplant the United States, Lee responded: "Of course. Why not? How could [the Chinese] not aspire to be number one in Asia and, in time, the world?"

One clear example of how the history deficit can be dangerous becomes apparent when considering America's dealings in the Middle East. If the president who takes office in 2017 were preparing to engage the leaders of Israel and the leading Arab nations on the Israeli-Palestinian conundrum, what might he or she ask the applied historians? A good start would be to ask them what have been the most significant U.S. policies and actions in the region in recent decades and how key players in Israel, the Palestinian territories, Jordan, Saudi Arabia, Egypt, and Iran interpret and remember those decisions. As Dennis Ross has noted, while U.S. leaders are usually ignorant of our previous actions in the Middle East, "those in the region know the history very well." How does the experience they have inherited from the past differ from ours? What lessons have they drawn from U.S. behavior?

A fifth type of assignment for applied historians is to pose and answer "what if?" questions designed to analyze past decision-making. Addressing such questions requires disciplined counterfactual reasoning. While many mainstream historians have voiced reservations about counterfactual analysis, this method lies at the heart of every historical account. As one of us argued in *Virtual History*, "it is a logical necessity when asking questions about causation to pose 'but for' questions, and to try to imagine what would have happened if our supposed cause had been absent."[6]

When assessing the relative importance of various possible causes of World War I, historians make judgments about what would have happened in the absence of these factors. Methods developed for doing this systematically can be employed by applied historians in considering current policy choices. Thus, President Obama's successor could ask his Council of Historical Advisers to replay 2013. What if Obama had opted to enforce the "red line" in Syria against the Assad regime, rather than delegating the removal of chemical weapons from Syria to the Russian government? And what if, in January 2014, the EU had not offered Ukraine an economic association agreement that was clearly designed to pull Kiev westward? Would President Putin still have intervened militarily in Ukraine?

A sixth kind of question for the Council of Historical Advisers would be of a fundamentally strategic nature. Is the United States in irreversible decline? Can it overcome the challenges facing it to lead a new "American century," or will the coming decades see the steady erosion of American power? Applied historians would begin by noting the recurring streak in American political culture of what Sam Huntington labeled "declinism." Many people were convinced that the United States was being overtaken by the Soviet Union in the late 1950s and 1960s, or by Japan in the 1980s. But in none of the earlier cases had the majority of Americans lost faith in the American Dream: the belief that if one works hard and plays by the rules, one's children will have more opportunities and a higher standard of living than their parents. In the past generation, as middle-class incomes have stagnated, that belief has been eroded. Bismarck defined a statesman as "a politician who thinks of his grandchildren." It is unclear whether the current American political system would allow such a statesman to enact the farsighted policies required to address the growing problem of intergeneration inequity—or indeed to be elected in the first place. The current generation is the first in the history of the United States to have asked, in essence, "What have our children and grandchildren ever done for us?" A truly visionary president would revive the importance of our posterity as the most important constituent of a well-governed republic.

Finally, a more speculative assignment, but still a vital one, would be to ask the council: "What unlikely but possible strategic upheavals might we face in the medium-term?"

- Will ISIS buy or steal a nuclear weapon?

- Will Chinese and Japanese forces clash in the East China Sea, sparking a wider war?

- Will the Saudi royal family be deposed?

- Will the European Union disintegrate?

- Will Russia invade a Baltic state?

While some of these scenarios may seem far-fetched, recall this time six years ago: How many pundits would have predicted the timing or speed of the Arab Spring, or that Syria would now lie in ruins? Two and a half years ago, how many believed it probable that Vladimir Putin would invade Crimea, that his proxies would shoot down a Dutch airliner, or that he would commit combat forces to Syria?

Of course, building future scenarios is part of what intelligence agencies do. Yet, currently, historians play a very small part in this process. Applied historians do not have crystal balls. But they do have certain advantages over those who would try to answer such questions with models and regression analysis. They know that dramatic events that were dismissed as implausible before the fact are in hindsight frequently described as inevitable. Their study of previous sharp discontinuities encourages a "historical sensibility" that is attuned to the long-term rhythms, strategic surprise, and daring *coups de main* that run through history.

This historical sensibility can prove invaluable. One applied historian, now well-known for discerning and profiting from long-term historical cycles in markets, developed so much of an historical sensibility while writing a doctoral dissertation on the relationship between commodities and the grand strategy of the British Empire that he was able to anticipate Iraq's seizure of Kuwait's oil fields, a full two years before Saddam made his move.

For too long, history has been disparaged as a "soft" subject, often by social scientists offering spuriously hard certainty. We believe it is time for a new and rigorous applied history to close America's history deficit. Not only do we want to see it incorporated into the Executive Office of the President, alongside the economic expertise that has so long been seen as indispensable to the executive branch. We also want to see it develop as a discipline in its own right in our universities, beginning at Harvard.

Harvard's Applied History Project is taking a "big tent" approach to revitalizing applied history in the academy and promoting its use in government, business, and other sectors of society. We stake no claim to inventing the concept: indeed, we trace its origins back at least to Thucydides and acknowledge that it had been a major strand in mainstream history until recent decades. We make no claim to exclusivity: indeed, we applaud colleagues—and mentors—such as Sir Michael Howard of Oxford or Paul Kennedy of Yale, whose contributions in this domain we celebrate and hope to emulate.

We encourage journalists to ask candidates for the presidency how they intend to eliminate the history deficit in American policy making. The slogan "America First" has a bad history. A better slogan—which has no past to speak of in the United States—might be "History First."

Graham Allison is Director of the Belfer Center for Science and International Affairs and Douglas Dillon Professor of Government at Harvard's John F. Kennedy School of Government. As "Founding Dean" of the modern Kennedy School, under his leadership, from 1977 to 1989, a small, undefined program grew twenty-fold to become a major professional school of public policy and government. Dr. Allison has served as Special Advisor to the Secretary of Defense under President Reagan and as Assistant Secretary of Defense for Policy and Plans under President Clinton, where he coordinated DOD strategy and policy towards Russia, Ukraine, and the other states of the former Soviet Union. He has been awarded the Department of Defense's highest civilian award, the Distinguished Public Service Medal, twice: first by Secretary Cap Weinberger and second by Secretary Bill Perry. He served as a member of the Defense Policy Board for Secretaries Weinberger, Carlucci, Cheney, Aspin, Perry, and Cohen. Dr. Allison's first book, *Essence of Decision: Explaining the Cuban Missile Crisis* (1971), ranks among the all-time bestsellers with more than 450,000 copies in print. His latest book (2013), *Lee Kuan Yew: The Grand Master's Insights on China, the United States and the World* (co-authored with Robert Blackwill), has been a bestseller in the U.S. and abroad. His previous book, *Nuclear Terrorism: The Ultimate Preventable Catastrophe*, is now in its third printing and was selected by the *New York Times* as one of the "100 most notable books of 2004." He is a member of the Aspen Strategy Group.

Niall Ferguson is a senior fellow of the Hoover Institution, Stanford, and a senior fellow of the Center for European Studies, Harvard. He is also a visiting professor at Tsinghua University, Beijing, and the Diller-von Furstenberg Family Foundation Distinguished Scholar at the Nitze School of Advanced International Studies in Washington, DC. He has written fourteen books, including *The House of Rothschild, Empire, The War of the World, The Ascent of Money, The Great Degeneration*, and *Kissinger, 1923-1968: The Idealist*. His 2011 feature-length film *Kissinger* won the New York International Film Festival's prize for best documentary. His PBS series *The Ascent of Money* won the International Emmy for best documentary. His many prizes and awards include the Benjamin Franklin Prize for Public Service (2010), the Hayek Prize for Lifetime Achievement (2012), and the Ludwig Erhard Prize for Economic Journalism (2013). He writes a weekly column for the *London Sunday Times* and the *Boston Globe*.

[1] Neustadt, Richard E., and Ernest R. May. 1986. *Thinking in Time: The Uses of History for Decision-Makers*. Florence, MA: Free Press.

[2] Ross, Dennis. 2015. *Doomed to Succeed: The U.S.-Israel Relationship from Truman to Obama*. New York: Farrar, Straus and Giroux.

[3] Bernanke, Ben. 2015. *The Courage to Act: A Memoir of a Crisis and Its Aftermath*. New York: W.W. Norton & Company.

[4] Reinhart, Carmen M., and Kenneth S. Rogoff. February 3, 2009. "What Other Financial Crises Tell Us." *Wall Street Journal*.

[5] Allison, Graham. July 30, 2014. "Just How Likely Is Another World War?" *The Atlantic*.

[6] Ferguson, Niall, editor. 1997. *Virtual History: Alternatives and Counterfactuals*. London: Picador.

"The burden of being the most powerful nation puts a unique responsibility on the U.S. president's shoulders to navigate the world through the upheavals that come ever more frequently and more urgently."

—JOHN SAWERS

Global Challenges 2017:
What Are The Threats Ahead?

John Sawers
Chairman and Partner
Macro Advisory Partners

Turbulent, unpredictable, volatile, complex. These adjectives often describe today's world. The next U.S. president won't have the "in-tray from hell" that President Obama inherited—two counter-insurgency wars, a global financial crisis, and an economic recession. But she or he will inherit the presidency against a backdrop of sharp domestic division and diminished U.S. power.

Seven Features of the World of 2017

Reduced U.S./Western dominance. In the 1980s, the G7 countries contributed close to 70 percent of global GDP. In 2015, it had fallen to 47 percent. The International Monetary Fund projects it will fall further, to 44 percent in 2021. Politically, the U.S. is no longer the global hegemon that it was from 1990-2008. The forces of globalization and integration are still in place—technology, trade in services as well as goods, global finance, greater movement of people and jobs. But the world is more splintered, with regional powers acting more independently in politics, security, and business. We live in a matrix world with forces of integration operating alongside forces of fragmentation and protectionism. As a consequence, U.S. leadership is much harder to assert.

Reduced U.S. confidence. Partly in reaction to Iraq and Afghanistan, the U.S. has become much more cautious in projecting power. U.S. leadership under Obama, reflecting public opinion, has been circumspect, at times hesitant. Russia (in Ukraine and Syria) and China (in the South China Sea) have used their new investments in military capability to project military power in a way not seen since the Soviet invasion of Afghanistan. The U.S. has not yet found a way to respond to this new assertiveness. The "reset with Russia" was short lived, and Russia's hybrid warfare poses a new challenge to NATO. The "pivot to Asia" has little to show for it so far.

Elsewhere, Obama's deliberate contrast to Bush's use of U.S. power has not been a strategic success. The Arab Spring was over-hyped by the media, but if there was an opportunity for change, then it was missed. "Leading from behind" in Libya left behind chaos. Nonintervention in Syria has proved more costly in human terms than intervention did in Iraq. Europe bears some of the responsibility for all this. Its preoccupation with its own problems hasn't helped, though where U.S. leadership has been on show (e.g., sanctions against Russia over Ukraine), European solidarity has been greater than some would have expected. Valuable progress on Iran and Cuba are positives in Obama's record, but they aren't the core of Obama's legacy to his successor.

A global economy that is muddling through. Global growth has slipped to below 2.5 percent, which is unsatisfactory, but not as bad as it might be. The global financial system is back on its feet, though still with pockets of vulnerability (e.g., Italian banks). The U.S. has resumed its traditional role as the driver of global growth, but that growth will be anemic. The Eurozone has only just returned to 2008 levels of output and is underperforming. The Brexit decision has set back the UK economy and will lead to several years of uncertainty affecting the rest of the EU too. Japan hasn't yet shrugged off its 25 years of sclerosis. China's slowdown is probably greater than shown in Chinese statistics, and the scale of Chinese debt (237 percent of GDP) is a vulnerability. Oil producers are still struggling to adjust to the halving of the oil price, and few countries—India is the main exception—have converted the dividend from lower energy costs into higher growth.

Huge political change in Western democracies. In the 1990s, the "third way" was the new politics on the center-left. "Compassionate conservatism" emerged in the 2000s on the center-right. Both sought the center ground as the path to electoral success. The Tea Party in the United States challenged that orthodoxy but may now itself be overtaken. Eight years after the global financial crash, we face a rising tide of anti-establishment sentiment as the global economy fails to deliver benefits for the average Western employee. Worse, there is a growing under-class of people, many with college degrees, who live precariously on the fringe of the economy. All this is driving politics on the left (Sanders, Corbyn, Syriza, Podemos) and right (Trump, Le Pen, Wilders, the Five Star Movement, AfD) toward simplicity, populism, and nationalism. The West does not have its own house in order.

The return of Big Man politics internationally. In both autocracies and democracies, political power is shifting from institutions and political parties back to individuals. Putin, Xi, Erdogan, Modi, Abe, Zuma, and Trump are all examples. They concentrate power on themselves, suppress sources of opposition both within and outside their political organizations, and often see themselves as above criticism and legal constraint. They can act capriciously, with little notice. There are exceptions— Latin America is moving away from such politics. But the rest of the World seems to aspire to Chavez-type leadership and Peronist-type movements just as Chavez-ism is dying and Peronism is, for now at least, marginalized. Maybe the rise of composed, politically strong female leaders, like Angela Merkel, Theresa May, and Hillary Clinton, will challenge the ugly old politics many countries are reverting to.

Technology is continuing to act as an engine of progress and also a disruptor of business and society. We may think our lives have already been transformed by technology. But technology-driven change is only going to accelerate. To take one example, fracking can be credited with halving the oil price as it broke Saudi Arabia's role as swing producer and ended the oil cartel. Data analytics is massively improving efficiency and safety; however, it is also going to change notions of accountability and privacy. Artificial Intelligence will challenge white-collar jobs in the way robotics displaced blue-collar workers. Technology is a great equalizer at one level, but the new media it has spawned has fueled populism and undermined representative democracy. In the economy, technology is a driver of inequality: the benefits go to the few, and the savings generated come from the many. And technology is morally neutral: it is used by the enemies of society just as much as for society's benefit. Cyber crime now outweighs all other types of criminality. And cyber warfare threatens to change how hostilities between states are settled.

The Islamic world is a mess, with consequences for Western societies. While most regions of the world move gradually forward, the Islamic world, especially the Arab world, remains riven by poor governance and sectarian disputes. Worse, the resulting disorder projects itself outward through terrorist organizations and migration pressures, which impact basic security in Western countries. Furthermore, the extremist groups seem to be deliberately provoking a violent backlash in order to increase tensions and polarize opinion.

Four Themes for the Next President's Foreign Policy

So, against this very difficult backdrop, what should be the new U.S. president's priorities when he or she takes office next January?

1. Restore Western unity and respect for U.S. leadership.

Power in the world reflects strength at home. The West has been weakened by poor economic performance and domestic division. The U.S. political system is proving to be dysfunctional. The European Union is too remote from its citizens and is struggling to match its big achievements, like the common currency and stabilizing Central Europe, with the political structures required. Japan is showing signs of a new assertiveness—a mixed blessing maybe, but one that needs to be harnessed to wider Western interests.

No single country is responsible for the health of the transatlantic relationship or the wider Western alliance. But the U.S. president has the unique ability to galvanize and lead. While Western leaders are overly consumed by second-order domestic political issues—David Cameron was a perfect example—the rise of illiberal democracies and "managed" market economies is posing a major threat to the West's interests and values. Far from 1989 marking the undisputed triumph of plural politics and market economics, the Western system is now facing a challenge just as serious as the challenges from fascism in the 1930s and communism in the Cold War.

A reassertion of our values and goals is required, coupled with tangible commitments to defense, security, rule of law, free markets, and human rights to underpin the Western system. That means the new U.S. president would be wise to invest in an effort with Europe, Japan, and other like-minded allies, like South Korea, Canada, and Australia, with the aim of the West once again becoming the lode star for countries in Latin America, Asia, and Africa. This would also mean making difficult decisions to restore health to America's democracy and to meet the reasonable expectations of America's allies (e.g., climate change).

2. Put great-power relations on a stable footing.

Relations between the great powers require active management and clear strategic thinking. The era of U.S. domination has proved brief, and we have to adjust.

The U.S.-China relationship is central to global stability, and the United States has done a good job in recent years in building a balanced relationship, drawing China into the international economic system while maintaining America's leading role in Asia. It was easier while Deng Xiaoping's "hide and bide" approach prevailed. Xi Jinping has set that aside and is asserting China's power in Asia—in many ways a natural consequence of China's economic clout but deeply troubling to East and Southeast Asian nations.

Accommodating China's rise is the central challenge in the world. But that requires some difficult decisions on how power in Asia can be shared. Containing—or "balancing" as some scholars put it—China's rise is a path to confrontation. But failing to stand up to China simply leads them to plough on inexorably, as they have done in the last decade in the South China Sea and in the cyber realm.

China's behavior will be shaped by U.S. policies and actions. However hard to envisage, a cooperative relationship is more likely to generate a win-win result than a competitive relationship. The latter is likely to end in spheres of influence and the U.S. being pushed slowly backward in Asia. As well as all the sectoral dialogues with China, the new U.S. president needs a trusted envoy to explore with those close to Xi how global stability and security is to be managed over the next twenty years and beyond.

One specific challenge facing U.S.-China relations is North Korea. The problem will assume a new order of magnitude during the next president's term in office, when Pyongyang will be able to deliver a nuclear warhead to the continental United States. That is a threat that would be hard for any U.S. leader to abide. Missile defense may provide some protection, but it would only be a matter of time before North Korea's capability would overwhelm U.S. defenses. If North Korea has to be forcibly disarmed, that is likely to require the removal of the Kim Jong-un regime. China has no liking for Kim, but has always preferred backing him over applying serious pressure to disarm. An understanding regarding North Korea at the highest level will be required, and that will pose enormously difficult decisions for both the U.S. and Chinese leaders.

Russia is not the same order of challenge as China, nor is it really any longer a great power, except in terms of the damage it can bring about. But that should be enough reason for the next president to develop a clear strategy for Russia and not just deal with Russia when it creates a problem or is needed (e.g., in the UN Security Council). Better and clearer communications will be needed, especially in private. Ukraine is an example of a crisis that, in part, grew out of the lack of a trusted top-level relationship between Putin and Obama and Russia's false assessment of what was happening on the ground. There has been better strategic-level communication over Syria. We need to manage relations with Russia carefully while its power gradually declines, not rub its nose in it—even though Russia would delight in doing that if the roles were reversed.

The next president will need to invest much time managing great-power relations. Decision-making in Beijing and Moscow is heavily centralized, and the right signals have to be driven through the administrations in all three capitals to move away from a presumption of military confrontation and hardball diplomacy. We may have to fall back on that at times, but it would be self-fulfilling if that is our starting assumption.

3. Promote economic growth at home and abroad.

Rising prosperity contributes to stability. It integrates more nations into the global economy and, within countries, it promotes a rising middle class and better balanced societies. All these encourage moderation in leaders' behavior and increase the scope for win-win solutions to interstate problems.

The world is still recovering from the financial crash. Emerging markets seemed to fare better than Western markets after 2008, but that was largely because of a massive injection of credit into China's economy, which has contributed to its current slowdown. Western economies are more robust than ten years ago, and our financial systems are more resilient. New technologies come overwhelmingly from the West and provide a new competitive edge. Interest rates are at an all-time low. But global growth has slowed, and the decline in energy prices seems to have held back growth more than it has stimulated it.

Figure 1. Percent Change in Real GDP in the World, Select Countries, and Country Groupings (1990-2015)

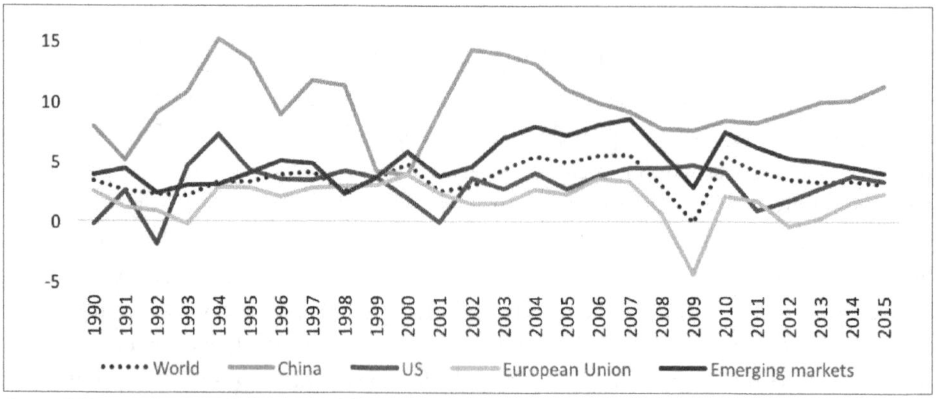

Source: IMF World Economic Outlook, April 2016

Protectionist demands in the West are fueled by concern that the globalized economy has led to a stagnation in median Western incomes and a rise in the power of countries that are not natural allies of the West. No leader can just ignore those concerns. But the means being pursued—both candidates have turned their backs on free trade—is likely to further set back global growth at a time when the global economy badly needs more stimulus. It is hard to see how the Transatlantic Trade and Investment Partnership and the Trans-Pacific Partnership can survive if they aren't concluded under Obama. But the next president should strive to keep them alive.

Figure 2. Year-Over-Year Percentage Change in Global Trade Volumes (January 2001-May 2016)

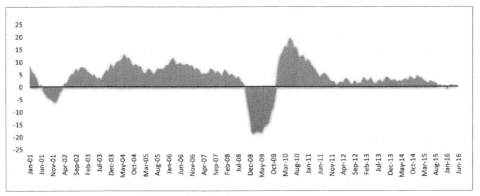

Source: CPB Netherlands Bureau for Economic Policy Analysis

The next U.S. president needs to more broadly prioritize economic growth, and ensure that the benefits of growth are felt by all. This is needed to reestablish the political health of Western countries and also to bind emerging-market countries into the U.S.-led international system. But that system too needs to be adjusted to reflect the new realities. The emergence of the Asian Infrastructure Investment Bank was a result of the U.S. Congress's failure to adjust voting powers in the IMF and World Bank. When U.S. leadership is inflexible, as it was in this case, other powers will find workarounds, and the U.S. in the longer term will lose out.

4. Help restore stability and build a better order in the Islamic world.

Much though we would like to reduce our engagement and devote time to more rewarding regions, like Latin America and Asia, the Middle East and the surrounding region from Pakistan to Morocco will continue to command our attention.

The cocktail offered by the region is a lethal one, more so than eight years ago:

- A failure of governance in much of the Arab World with serious weaknesses too in Iran and Pakistan

- Heightening sectarian and ethnic tensions, and proxy conflicts between Saudi Arabia and Iran

- The emergence in the post-Arab Spring of wide areas of disorder driving millions from their homes, destabilizing neighboring countries and the European Union, and creating a new generation of disaffected and under-educated Muslim youth

- Terrorist groups exploiting the ungoverned spaces to control territory, build their support, and orchestrate terror attacks across the region and in the West

- The fall in oil and gas revenues leading to huge budget deficits in countries that had recently raised public spending to counter discontent

- A poor work ethic, resistance to women in the workplace, weak bureaucratic capacity

What signs of hope are there?

There are some. ISIS's progress has been stalled, and the space available to them in Syria, Iraq, and Libya is being squeezed. Saudi Arabia's deputy crown prince has set out a new and encouraging vision for his country, and he now needs help to fulfill it in a way that doesn't lead to expectations being raised and then dashed. Iran's revolution is now middle-aged, and the country's politics are gradually moving away from the ayatollahs and the securocrats. The popular response to the coup attempt in Turkey shows a resistance to military rule despite Erdogan's suppression of political freedoms. Pakistan has edged back from chaos, and a rapprochement with India is once again conceivable. The Arab monarchies have shown that consent can be maintained if populations benefit from public services and have opportunities to work. And in Tunisia and Morocco, elected governments are showing that—within bounds—democracy can slowly be built in the region.

The Middle East is no longer about the Israel-Palestine issue, if it ever really was. There is a much deeper dysfunction that requires American attention if the leaders in the region are to find a way forward. There are building blocks to work with, and America remains the dominant influence at both leadership and popular levels.

Part of the purpose of presidential engagement is damage limitation. But America will live to regret it if benign neglect, born of war weariness and greater energy independence, leads to even more regional turmoil.

Conclusion

Today's world is much less congenial to Western interests than the one that existed when President Bill Clinton assumed office. Most of the changes over the last twenty-four years have made life more difficult for a U.S. leader. But I am conscious that the priorities I have set out for the next U.S. president are not vastly different. Yes, there are specific threats, like climate change, migration, and cyber warfare, that have to be addressed, and there are regions of the world, like Latin America, where there may be some early wins. But a major shift away from a balanced global approach that includes building security, promoting prosperity, and—where we can—protecting fundamental freedoms, will constitute an unnecessary retreat by the U.S.

As we survey the messy and complex world situation that the next president inherits, let's not forget that the United States remains by far the world's most powerful and dynamic nation. American leadership is often criticized, resented, or resisted. But its absence creates much greater problems than its presence. The burden of being the most powerful nation puts a unique responsibility on the U.S. president's shoulders to navigate the world through the upheavals that come ever more frequently and more urgently.

Sir John Sawers is Chairman and Partner of Macro Advisory Partners, a firm that provides its clients with the strategic understanding needed to navigate the intersection of global markets, geopolitics, and government policy. He joined MAP in early 2015. John completed his public service career as Chief of the British Secret Intelligence Service (MI6) for five years, 2009-2014. As Chief he modernised the way the Service works and created a more open approach to public accountability, as well as leading it through a period of high terrorist threat and international political upheaval. Prior to leading MI6, he was the UK's Ambassador to the United Nations (2007-2009), Political Director of the Foreign Office (2003-2007), Special Representative in Iraq (2003), Ambassador to Cairo (2001-2003) and Foreign Policy Adviser to Prime Minister Tony Blair (1999-2001). He studied at the universities of Nottingham, St Andrews, and Harvard. John is, in addition, a Non-Executive Director of BP, a Visiting Professor at King's College London, a Senior Fellow of the Royal United Services Institute and a Governor of the Ditchley Foundation.

Part 2

A NEW SYSTEM FOR NEW CHALLENGES

CHAPTER 3

Speculation on Economic/Political Consequences of a British Withdrawal from the EU

Leah Joy Zell
Lizard Investors LLC

CHAPTER 4

Government for a Digital Economy— In a Time of Deeply Intertwined Economic and National Security Imperatives

Zoë Baird
Markle Foundation

CHAPTER 5

Reshaping National Security Institutions for Emerging Technology

Christopher Kirchhoff
U.S. Department of Defense

"A union is only as strong as its weakest link."

— LEAH JOY ZELL

Speculation on Economic/Political Consequences of a British Withdrawal from the EU

Leah Joy Zell
CEO
Lizard Investors LLC

The result of the June 23rd referendum was a shock for those who expected the status quo to prevail. It is early days yet. We are at the beginning of a process with numerous variables and feedback loops. Divorces rarely come out the way the warring parties envision at the start, and they often settle when exhaustion sets in, on terms that would have been previously unacceptable. No predictions can be made at this stage with a high degree of confidence; even reconciliation is possible.

The outcome for both parties is nonetheless of momentous significance. The UK is the fifth largest economy in the world and second only to Germany in Europe. The prospect of its withdrawal from a project whose roots go back to the post-World War II global economic architecture heralds a major shift away from established norms. All applications to the EU since inception have been for inclusion. Brexit would set a precedent in the other direction, which automatically raises the question of who might come next.

Assuming Brexit indeed occurs, this paper does not dwell on the paths the parties might take to achieve divorce, which can be fiendishly complex and have already garnered a great deal of press. Rather, it focuses on potential longer-term consequences in the political economy realm, which may unfold as the negotiations occur.

The paper's first hypothesis is that London's dominance as a global financial capital will persist, giving the UK more leverage than the doomsday scenarios predict. By contrast, much of UK industry is deeply embedded in European supply chains, making it harder to extricate those businesses from their trading partners on the continent without major disruption. Ironically, the constituencies who voted to remain are likely to be most shielded from the negative ramifications of independence, while the constituency who supported Brexit will bear a disproportionate share of the pain. The second hypothesis of the paper is that Europe faces intractable problems stemming from the single currency that Brexit did not cause. However, an EU without the UK at the table leaves Germany subject to burdens it may not be willing to bear, and uniquely vulnerable to a potential dissolution of the Eurozone. As such, the spillover effects of Brexit pose a greater risk to global stability than the UK economic impact. Finally, the paper posits that the United States has an important role to play in bringing the parties together and acting as a counterbalance within the transatlantic alliance in support of the global economy and the liberal world order.

The UK Crown Jewel: London and the Financial Services Sector

London has been a massive beneficiary of globalization. For decades after World War II ended, London bore the marks of privation. Behind the facades of pretty Victorian terrace houses, shilling meters rationed heat and hot water ran at most a few hours a day. No one below the age of forty remembers that. As the world has grown more interconnected, London's unique advantages have returned it to one of the leading global cities, with echoes of the grandeur it enjoyed when British colonialism was at its zenith. The engine of its renaissance has been the financial services sector, and its denizens voted overwhelmingly to remain. Will its prominence survive Brexit?

Financial services account for 10 percent of UK GDP, the highest share among the G7. Associated professional services, such as legal, accounting, and consulting, represent an additional 5 percent of GDP. UK financial services contribute more to both corporate and income tax revenues than any other sector. Including insurance, the UK is the world's largest exporter of financial services, producing a trade surplus of around 3.5 percent of GDP. The London Stock Exchange is the most liquid in Europe and has the largest number of foreign listed companies. Four of the ten largest global law firms are based in London. Several of the largest sovereign wealth funds call London their second home, including Abu Dhabi, Singapore, and Kuwait.

The City of London reports the UK's market share in global financial markets as follows:[1]

Market	Share	Rank
Non-ferrous metals trading	90%	#1
International bond trading	70%	#1
Ship-broking—tankers	50%	#1
Derivatives (OTC interest rate)	46%	#1

Foreign exchange trading	37%	#1
Marine insurance premiums	19%	#1
Cross-border bank lending	19%	#1
Hedge fund assets	18%	#2
Private equity	12%	#2

While the EU share of this business is significant, the city's dominance in key financial verticals is only partially due to EU proximity, and less tied than people think. The insurance sector's export trade with the EU is only 20 percent of the total. The EU figures more prominently in the UK's export of other financial services, at 40 percent of the total, but its importance is expected to decline in relative terms due to the lack of growth in Europe.[2] Trading in the Chinese RMB is a good example of the globalized nature of financial services, and the centrality of the City of London. Whereas ten years ago RMB foreign exchange was irrelevant, it is now the fourth largest currency traded on ICAP's EBS platform, with London capturing 50-plus percent of market share outside of Hong Kong and the Chinese mainland.[3]

It is hard to envision that Brexit by itself could cause London lasting damage because the city's comparative advantages are difficult to dislodge. The deep pools of talent concentrated in the UK capital will not be easy to replicate elsewhere. Language is another key factor, with English preferred by global business elites. English commercial law underpins many of the complex OTC derivatives and swap trades in which London specializes. Time zone also favors London, which can transact with Asia in the morning and the United States in the afternoon. Good schools, luxury housing, restaurants, retail establishments, a rich array of cultural offerings, and a welcoming environment for the cosmopolitan elite—who hail from "everywhere and nowhere"—complete the picture.

The continent is challenged to come up with a similar offering. Were there a credible European champion, it would have made greater inroads before the Brexit vote. Paris has a reputation for bureaucracy and "soak the rich" politics that incentivized 250,000 French citizens to decamp across the Channel. French social charges, approximately 34 percent higher than those levied in the UK per equivalent employee, make setting up shop in the French capital prohibitively expensive for enterprises that need not be there. In general, labor laws across Europe are inflexible and high cost. Places like Dublin, Warsaw, and Luxembourg have advantages for niche purposes but lack the infrastructure, network benefits, and overall quality of life that make London a magnet for talent.[4] Earlier this year, the London Stock Exchange and its German counterpart, Deutsche Börse, announced plans to merge. It is telling that Brexit has accelerated the deal, as opposed to killing it.[5]

No doubt, the EU will use access to its markets by UK financial service firms as a bargaining chip in the upcoming negotiations. Banks worldwide, facing lower profitability since the financial crisis and looking for ways to lower costs, will move some operations out of London to cheaper locations where they are already licensed. The European Central Bank has pushed for years to transfer the clearing of Euro-denominated trades to the Eurozone. It is unlikely that the EU will grant London "passporting" rights—allowing UK-based firms to offer financial services on the continent on the same terms as now—without a fight. The overriding conclusion, however, is that there is currently no viable European alternative to London as a global financial capital.

British policy makers can shape the outcome by favorable regulatory, tax, and immigration policies, or restrictive measures that make the city less hospitable to internationally mobile plutocrats. Major changes are unlikely to unfold overnight. What will be of greatest importance to London's prosperity over time will be the trajectory of globalization. Anything that impedes the free movement of goods, capital, and labor is negative for cities claiming world status. Should Europe's economy grow at a substantially faster pace than the UK, and/or its regulatory climate evolve in a business-friendly direction, financiers will eventually pick up and move. For now, the rich and their acolytes are likely to stay put.

A Tale of Two Countries

Outside of the financial services sector, the UK's bargaining position is more complicated. Britain runs a trade deficit with the rest of the EU, which implies that its fellow EU members have more incentive to make a deal. But exports to the UK comprise 5 percent of EU GDP ex-UK, whereas the UK's exports to the continent are 15 percent of UK GDP, implying that the British economy is three times more dependent on Europe for trade than vice versa.

In the short term, the biggest risks to the UK economy involve investment and consumer confidence. The UK has 7 percent of the world's foreign direct investment, second only to the United States. Half of that investment has come from the EU.[6] Given the uncertainty surrounding trade negotiations, the path of least resistance for global corporates post-Brexit is to put future investment decisions on hold. A recent survey conducted by IHS Markit indicates that Britain's economy is slowing at the fastest pace since the height of the financial crisis, with both manufacturing and services in contraction. So concerns regarding an upcoming recession in the

UK appear well founded, and policy makers will struggle to remove the uncertainty weighing on economic activity.

The auto industry illustrates the point. The UK car industry employs 800,000 people in places like Sunderland in the north and Brigend in Wales. Easy access to the EU has fueled its development, with 57 percent of production going to the continent.[7] Japanese manufacturers focus on low-volume models and operate at thin margins. Ford and BMW make engines that are shipped to factories in Germany and elsewhere for cars that are subsequently sent back to the UK to be sold. All have plants elsewhere where production could be moved, especially for newer models.

Countries outside the EU are subject to a 10 percent tariff on automobiles, which if levied, would render a meaningful percentage of current UK production uneconomic. Germany might be eager to grant the UK trade concessions on automobiles because Britain is the largest export market for its luxury cars. But the other 26 countries will want to extract their pound of flesh in exchange for approving a deal. Unwinding a 40-plus-year relationship takes time. In the interim, jobs in the UK hinterlands are at risk, not just in automobile production. This will hurt precisely those constituencies that voted for exit.

Europe Has Troubles of Its Own Without Brexit

An economically vibrant EU would have been harder for the UK to leave. In point of fact, the IMF projects lackluster growth for Europe—1.6 percent in 2016 and 1.4 percent next year. The aggregate figures mask sharp differences in the economic status of individual countries and industries, wherein lies the problem.

Broadly viewed, European corporates underperform their Anglo-Saxon peers. An *Economist* article in early July observed that "after a decade of stagnation the continent's firms have suffered an alarming decline in their global clout." Among the 50 most valuable firms in the world, as measured by stock market capitalization, seven hail from Europe, compared with seventeen ten years ago. The United States has thirty-one firms, and China now has eight. Only Nestlé leads its sector from Europe. The Brazilian-controlled beer company AB InBev made the cut because it happens to be listed in Belgium. Some of the disparity derives from higher multiples on U.S. public exchanges, but aggregate profits of the top 500 European firms are 50-65 percent smaller than the same slice of corporate America.[8]

The reasons behind this underperformance are legion, familiar, and mostly structural. Scale is a factor. European corporates lack vast domestic markets comparable to their U.S. and Chinese peers. Airbus is half as large as Boeing, and Siemens is a third the size of General Electric. Technocrats have promoted the virtues of cross-border mergers, but the end result is more often roll-ups of national champions than truly integrated enterprises. Nestlé is a global company, in both management and operations. As such, it is an outlier. Rigid labor markets, multiple languages, misguided anti-trust regimes, the absence of risk capital to support innovation, and a political climate less friendly to business all contribute to headwinds that impede efficiency and profits.

In particular, the dysfunctionality of Europe's banks highlights a key reason Europe's economy has struggled since the financial crisis. Post-2008, Europe never adequately recapitalized its banking system. The roots of the current malaise go back to the interrelated issues of Europe's overreliance on bank loans, fragmentation of the financial system, and the absence of deep, liquid markets. Banks provide over 80 percent of credit in Europe, compared to less than a third in the United States. Like Japan two decades ago, the response of the European regulators has been to procrastinate, in the hopes that the banking industry would grow out of its difficulties. As a result, surviving banks will need a greater injection of capital than might have been required five years ago, and weak institutions must be allowed to fail to reduce capacity. The question is who takes the losses. New bail-in rules developed in Brussels in 2014 mandate that bondholders and equity owners absorb the first 8 percent of liabilities. When those same stakeholders are private citizens as opposed to institutional investors, the consequence is a political crisis.

A union is only as strong as its weakest link. At the moment, the fault line runs down the spine of Italy. After three years of recession, its banking sector is groaning with bad loans estimated at €360 billion, or 20-plus percent of the country's GDP. Pier Carlo Padoan, Italian minister of economy and finance, a professorial figure who exudes nostalgia for his days as an academic, acknowledges that the nonperforming loans sit on bank balance sheets at roughly twice the price for which they could be sold to third parties. Deeply enmeshed in the political and social fabric of the country, domestic banks are the largest owners of Italian sovereign debt, and the main source of lending to an economy in which small entrepreneurial businesses make up 70 percent. Between a half and a third of the subordinated bonds issued by the banks are held by an estimated 60,000 retail investors.

Italian Prime Minister Matteo Renzi has unsuccessfully lobbied the EU to allow him to use government money to recapitalize Italy's banks. EU policy makers lost patience long ago with Italy's political culture and distrust Rome's resistance to imposing losses on private investors. Should Renzi defy Brussels and use public funds without following bail-in rules, the rating agencies may lower Italy's sovereign debt rating to junk; should he fail to fix the capital shortfall, he risks losing a critical constitutional referendum in December on which he has staked his political future. Italian bank shares are down over 50 percent year-to-date. No wonder the Italian index fell 12 percent on the day of the Brexit vote.[9]

Italy's travails were not caused by the Brexit referendum. But Europe's ability to deal with its economic difficulties has been compromised by the precedent of the UK decision to leave. The Euroskeptic Five Star Movement, which is gaining on Renzi's Democratic Party in the polls, has offered to hold an Italian referendum of its own on EU membership. It is not the only anti-establishment party looking for a fight. Almost half of the Italian population has said in polls that it favors exiting the union. Thankfully, the UK never adopted the euro. The Eurozone probably could have coped with the departure of a small economy like Greece. Italy is an entirely different ball of wax.

Germany's Dilemma

Angela Merkel's difficult job hasn't become any easier since the Brexit vote. Again, we are dealing with preexisting problems. The question is whether the UK's departure makes it easier or more difficult to resolve them. While Germany is the economic powerhouse of Europe, comprising 27 percent of the EU's GDP before Brexit and 34 percent after, its economic success rests on shaky pillars.

Germany's economy is export-oriented, sending 47 percent of its output abroad. The current account surplus, now approaching 9 percent of its economy and growing, exceeds that of China in absolute terms, notwithstanding the fact that China's economy is more than twice the size. There are two overriding explanations for why Germany runs such surpluses. First, the euro is set at a level below what would be equilibrium for the German economy on a standalone basis. As such, Germany is the greatest beneficiary of the currency union within the Eurozone. Second, conservative policies designed to protect German export competitiveness suppress domestic income and wages, leading to chronically weak demand.[10]

The consequence is that, along with goods and services, Germany exports deflation to its trading partners. In point of fact, the UK imports twice as much from

Germany as it exports back in return. In general, the trade surpluses of the northern European countries are mirrored in the deficits of their southern European partners. Smaller countries can get away with mercantilist practices, but imbalances of this magnitude by the world's fourth largest economy are *prima facie* unsustainable.

The European Union, as expressed through a shared currency, is the guarantor of Germany's prosperity and security. Should the Eurozone break up, the deutschmark would almost certainly appreciate by as much as one-third overnight, sending exports plummeting. The transition would be accompanied by extended bank holidays, capital controls, economic paralysis, and years of litigation. Brexit in this context presents Germany with an existential threat. Some form of fiscal burden sharing is a necessary antidote to the stresses that are tearing north and south apart. But Merkel and her finance minister, Wolfgang Schaüble, are accountable to an electorate neither comfortable with the responsibilities of great-power status nor accepting of the tradeoffs it brings. Accordingly, Schaüble has taken the "catch-22" position that Germany will only consider further integration when its partners' commit to structural reforms that will return their economies to financial health.

The Post-Brexit Transatlantic Balance of Power

In the first half of the twentieth century, two world wars were fought over how to incorporate Germany as a political and economic juggernaut within Europe. During the Cold War, division into the Bundesrepublik and the Deutsche Demokratische Republik placed the respective successor states into larger spheres of influence, which did not threaten neighboring powers. After the fall of the Soviet Union, reunited Germany has acted with acute sensitivity to its historical past and prioritized economic objectives over projecting political power. That distinction is no longer possible.

One year ago, Roger Cohen wrote a prescient op-ed for the *New York Times* titled "The German Question Redux." The crux of his essay revolves around the question, "Is German domination compatible with further European integration or will it prove a fracturing force?" He calls the euro a "poisoned chalice" and concludes that "overall [Merkel] ... has erred on the side of rigidity, austerity and responsibility lessons. German methods are good for Germans. But if Berlin now wants all Europeans to follow those methods, the Europe that offered postwar Germany a path to salvation will break apart."[11] If Germany's weight within the EU stirred resentments before the UK withdrawal, one can only speculate about what lies ahead.

There is a critical role for the United States to play in strengthening its ties with Berlin, while lending the UK support. The EU would be impoverished by Britain's departure, not least because the strongest voice for liberal economic policies will no longer participate in decision-making. At the same time, Germany loses the natural counterweight to its dominance of EU deliberations with the UK withdrawal. It is in the strongest interest of the United States to fill the vacuum, particularly as the parties renegotiate their future relations.

President Obama wrote an op-ed in the *Financial Times* after the Brexit referendum under the headline "America's Alliance with Britain and Europe Will Endure."[12] He focused his comments on NATO and security issues, which have not been disrupted. While defense is vitally important, so is the economic and political stability of the transatlantic sphere. The EU's core question is "more or less Europe." What is at stake goes beyond tariffs and visas to strike at the heart of the European project. The United States cannot resolve the internal conflicts of the Eurozone. But it can help minimize the spillover effects stemming from Brexit by encouraging both sides to arrive at a deal as close to status quo as they can sell to their respective electorates, including support for reconciliation should that possibility arise.

One last point bears mentioning. Those who voted for Brexit are disaffected. Stagnant wages, inequality, and slow growth have caused them to lose faith in globalization and to not trust their political leaders. Better economic prospects would turn the *Zeitgeist* around and restore confidence in the future. Many governments have greater room to borrow than suggested by prevailing orthodoxies. Record low interest rates make sovereign debt affordable, and central banks have implicitly agreed to fund the expenditures with quantitative easing. Immediately after the Brexit vote, Chancellor of the Exchequer George Osborne abandoned his government's commitment to balance the budget by 2020. Both candidates running for U.S. president look like spenders. Maybe the German political establishment will be the next to turn, especially if an SPD chancellor succeeds Angela Merkel. Should the rise of populist movements lead establishment politicians to embrace coordinated fiscal stimulus, then the message of Brexit will have gotten through.

Leah Joy Zell is a recognized expert in global investing, and a pioneer in the international small-cap category. Prior to establishing Lizard Investors LLC in 2008, she was a co-Founder and Partner at Wanger Asset Management, where she managed the Acorn International Fund and the international investment team from 1992-2005. Dr. Zell has been a board member of the Chicago Council on Global Affairs since 1998, where she currently serves as Treasurer and on the Executive Committee. Dr. Zell is a member of the New York Council on Foreign Relations, a Director of The Horton Trust Company LLC, on the Harvard Global Advisory Council, and a member of the investment committee of the Chicago Museum of Contemporary Art. Dr. Zell earned her Bachelor of Arts degree from Harvard College in 1971, graduating Magna Cum Laude and Phi Beta Kappa. In 1979, Dr. Zell received her PhD in Modern Social and Economic History from the Harvard Graduate School of Arts and Sciences. Dr. Zell earned her Chartered Financial Analyst (CFA®) designation in 1987.

[1] City of London Corporation. November 2013. *An Indispensable Industry: Financial Services in the UK.*

[2] Lea, Ruth. February 2015. "UK exports of insurance and financial services are crucially important, but EUR share is falling as growth disappoints." Economists for Britain.

[3] Stafford, Philip. July 20, 2016. "City Brokers Put Brave Face on Brexit." *Financial Times.*

[4] *Financial Times.* June 30, 2016. "Brexit and the City." Also see Stewart, James. June 30, 2016. "After 'Brexit,' Finding a New London for the Financial World to Call Home." *The New York Times.*

[5] This is not to say that the deal will go through. The EU regulators may delay or block completion. The plan had been to headquarter the combined firm in London, but locating it in Frankfurt may be a condition for approval.

[6] *The Economist.* July 9, 2016. "After the Brexit Vote: Rules and Britannia," 56.

[7] *The Economist.* July 23, 2016. "A Change of Gear," 44-45.

[8] *The Economist.* July 2, 2016. "From Clout to Rout," 55-57.

[9] See the excellent articles: Sanderson, Rachel, Alex Barker, and Claire Jones. July 10, 2016. "Italian Banks: Essential Repairs." *Financial Times*; Legorano, Giovanni. July 5, 2016. "Italy's Banks Loom as Europe's Next Crisis." *Wall Street Journal.*

[10] Bernanke, Ben. April 3, 2015. "Germany's Trade Surplus Is a Problem." Brookings Institution.

[11] Cohen, Roger. July 13, 2015. "The German Question Redux." *New York Times.*

[12] Obama, Barack. July 8, 2016. "America's Alliance with Britain and Europe Will Endure." *Financial Times.*

"Our nation seeks major change, and the next president can set in motion a transformative initiative to expand digital economy jobs and dramatically reshape how the government operates."

—ZOË BAIRD

Government For A Digital Economy—In A Time Of Deeply Intertwined Economic And National Security Imperatives

Zoë Baird
CEO and President
Markle Foundation

The private sector is transforming at record speed for the digital economy. As recently as 2008, when America elected President Obama, most large companies had separate IT departments, which were seen as just that—departments—separate from the heart of the business. Now, as wireless networks connect the planet, and entire companies exist in the cloud, digital technology is no longer viewed as another arrow in the corporate quiver, but rather the very foundation upon which all functions are built. This, then, is the mark of the digital era: in order to remain successful, modern enterprises must both leverage digital technology and develop a culture that values its significance within the organization.

For the federal government to help all Americans thrive in this new economy, and for the government to be an engine of growth, it too must enter the digital era. On a basic level, we need to improve the government's digital infrastructure and use technology to deliver government services better. But a government for the digital economy needs to take bold steps to embed these actions as part of a large and comprehensive transformation in how it goes about the business of governing. We should not only call on the "IT department" to provide tools, we must completely change the way we think about how a digital age government learns about the world, makes policy, and operates against its objectives.

Government today does not reflect the fundamental attributes of the digital age. It moves slowly at a time when information travels around the globe at literally the speed of light. It takes many years to develop and implement comprehensive policy in a world characterized increasingly by experimentation and iterative midcourse adjustments. It remains departmentally balkanized and hierarchical in an era of networks and collaborative problem solving. It assumes that it possesses the expertise necessary to make decisions while most of the knowledge resides at the edges. It is bogged down in legacy structures and policy regimes that do not take advantage of digital tools, and worse, create unnecessary barriers that hold progress back. Moreover, it is viewed by its citizens as opaque and complex in an era when openness and access are attributes of legitimacy.

Americans can see that the economy is changing, the government is not keeping up, and the government is not helping them find their place in the future. Only 20 percent of Americans would describe government programs as being well-run.[1]

The challenge of growing the digital economy is more than an issue of jobs and wages. It is a national security imperative as well. An effective digital-age government is essential to economic growth and the broad distribution of its benefits, which is a critical building block of America's power and influence in the world.

Pursuing the President's Digital Economy Strategy Through a Virtual Reorganization of Government

The next president needs to lead the change by creating a national digital economy strategy. Such a strategy begins with repositioning the federal government to act with the nimbleness and wisdom of the digital age, drawing on the resources and talent of the nation as a whole. This effort should include a "virtual reorganization" of government and the establishment of digital policy objectives that cross agency lines and engage the entire government to work toward their implementation with all the resources and expertise needed from both the domestic and national security communities.

A virtual reorganization does not require creating new agencies or an expansion of government. It requires innovating, collaborating, and coordinating in new ways. To jump-start this agenda, the president should create a White House Digital Economy Initiative to work with the cabinet—in conjunction with the White House offices that reach out to state and local governments, civil society, students, the private sector, unions, faith-based groups, and others—to articulate a path forward in the digital economy. The initiative would coordinate the development of the policy priorities and technology architecture of a virtual reorganization of government and a framework for its execution. And after one year, it should turn full responsibility over to the cabinet, where operation of the program belongs for the long term.[2]

The policy priorities and technology architecture, elaborated on below, should be designed to:

I. Grow jobs in the digital economy by:

  o closing the gap between the capacity of large and small businesses to participate in the digital economy, and

  o powering the skills-based labor market so people can get the skills they need for the growth jobs.

II. Evolve the role of government by:

  o shifting the culture of government operations, and

  o substantially changing how government works with the tech sector.

We must reimagine the structures and culture of government for a digital era. The rest of the country recognizes that we are at an inflection point. The government needs to catch up.

I. Growing Digital Economy Jobs

Closing the New Digital Divide

America is facing a growing gap in digital capabilities between large companies that have effectively digitized their operations and small and medium-sized enterprises (SMEs) that lack the money, resources, and skilled talent to do so. McKinsey estimates that U.S. digital industries have three times faster profit and margin growth and two times faster wage growth than the economy as a whole.[3] Boston Consulting Group estimates that UK digital industries grew 2.5 times faster than the economy as a whole between 2003 and 2013.[4]

That is a problem because large businesses are not America's primary job creators. SMEs are estimated to drive over 60 percent of new jobs created in the United States.[5] We need to spur a tremendous public-private collaboration to create digital platforms for SMEs, and from this initiative, a large number of good digital economy jobs.[6]

This digital divide—one in which businesses are lumped into technological haves and have-nots—has profound consequences. Digitization delivers new efficiencies, new opportunities, and even new customers. The effect is not linear; it is exponential.

SMEs would obviously benefit from these tools—but they are often cost prohibitive. When a major retailer uses census data to optimize product lines by region, or uses weather data to change inventory in real time, smaller stores simply cannot keep up.

The solution is a new digital economic agenda that gives SMEs access to the digital tools, technologies, and services driving the next wave of prosperity: online banking and payroll, supply chain management, data analytics, e-invoicing, and the many other basic means of digital intelligence and efficiency available to larger businesses that can power growth and thereby job creation.

There are many policies that the federal government can adopt across agencies to encourage SMEs to digitize, such as:

- Expand efforts by the Small Business Administration to train SMEs in, and incentivize them to use, digital tools that will optimize their business;

- Foster new public-private partnerships and collaborative efforts between SMEs (by providing infrastructure, tools, and investment) to help them better share data, analyze data, and gain better market intelligence;

- Open up more free federal data sources to SMEs and expand the work of the Commerce Data Service to serve small businesses; and

- Develop new approaches to data governance and privacy, examine the context of how the data is being used, and develop a set of guiding principles that build public trust.

Government can also enable SMEs to connect with rapidly growing global markets over the Internet, playing to our strengths in producing and exporting goods and, increasingly, services that could bring billions of potential new buyers to America's computer screens.

Research has shown that more than 90 percent of SMEs that sell goods and services on the eBay platform engage in overseas exports, compared with less than 5 percent of all U.S. SMEs.[7]

What's more, by 2022, China's middle class is expected to grow to an estimated 630 million people. These consumers will demand better health care, growing educational opportunities, and a cleaner environment—all services that the Chinese economy does not have the current capacity to supply at the necessary scale and quality, and which American companies can export.[8]

Public-private strategies can help develop digital platforms that reduce friction from customs, taxation, and shipping and help SMEs reach customers in every corner of the world.

Power the Skills-Based Labor Market

As America has moved into the digital economy, the labor market has changed—not just creating new types of jobs (e.g., programmers, developers, data analysts) but also rapidly changing the required skills in most other fields.

A recent study of labor market data by economists at the Pew Research Center, in association with the Markle Foundation, found that jobs that require highly skilled employees are growing at a significantly higher rate than jobs that require less education and training. What's more, the study found that higher-skill jobs (particularly jobs that require a high level of analytical or social skills) pay more than nonskilled jobs. In other words, skills have a direct link to higher-paying jobs. It's no surprise then that more than 54 percent of workers surveyed by Pew for the same study say that it will be "essential" for them to get more skills training throughout their career, and another 33 percent say it will be "important" to do so.[9]

The problem, though, is that while the *realities* of the labor market demonstrate the value of skills, it is enormously difficult to learn new skills in an affordable manner, demonstrate those skills to potential employers, or understand how to find jobs that require those specific skills. This is particularly true for the middle-skill worker who, like almost 70 percent of Americans, does not have a college degree.[10]

However, there is a solution. Digital platforms can further the transition toward a skills-based labor market by giving employers the opportunity to post open jobs in a transparent manner on the basis of the specific skills they need, not only diplomas obtained or previous jobs. This enables job seekers to demonstrate their skills and educators to see where the skills they teach are needed. Increasingly, these skills are both hard and soft skills, like critical thinking and collaborative problem solving. In such a labor market, those who do not have a college diploma, but do have the skills necessary for their job, become eligible to apply. Of course, it is also possible that we may see an increase in the number of people who, over a lifetime, acquire a college degree as well.

One example of such a platform is *Skillful*, an initiative of the Markle Foundation, in partnership with the state of Colorado and city of Phoenix and with LinkedIn, Arizona State University, edX, and local employers in Colorado and Phoenix. *Skillful* is a digital platform that provides job seekers a window into the growth jobs employers have available in their area, the skills needed and how to get them, easy access to local skills-training courses, and coaches to help them get on a better career path.

Platforms like *Skillful* are just beginning to develop. The federal government can accelerate their growth and national impact. The president should lead this effort—promoting the adoption of similar platforms and joining with employers, governors, educators, and local leaders who are creating skills-based labor markets.

In addition, the federal government ought to:

- Work together with other leading employers and associations toward developing more flexible, low-cost, and useful systems of skills credentials;

- Provide vouchers to take skills-training classes along with food stamps or unemployment checks—putting those who use government assistance in a better position to compete in the job market;

- Adjust financial aid systems to make them portable and flexible enough to encourage educational institutions to innovate;

- Use government buildings after hours and digital platforms for skills-training classes;

- Teach in-demand skills to federal employees (classes could even be open to the public);

- Incentivize government employees to act as mentors or coaches;

- Expand funding for apprenticeship programs between employers and schools, and work with unions to expand training and apprenticeship programs;

- Develop incentives for businesses to expand employee training, and encourage them to form partnerships with community colleges to offer affordable classes that teach skills tailored to a particular sector.

II. Evolving the Role of Government

Government itself must quickly begin to change the way it works or become increasingly irrelevant to everyday life. To make government more effective for the digital age, we must shift the culture of government operations and improve relations between the government and the tech sector.

Shift the Culture of Government Operations

To seize the opportunities presented by the digital economy, the federal government must embrace the management ethos of the digital economy: rewarding experimentation even if it can result in failure, decentralizing the processes, embracing open innovation and crowdsourcing of solutions, having competing teams working on the same problems, using data sources and advanced analytics to simulate a program's effectiveness and then optimize it for its target population, and testing different programs in different parts of the country to see which are most effective.

It is essential to create an effective regulatory environment for a digital economy, preserving the important values that regulations are meant to protect while updating the rules to reflect the modern digital era. Some regulations should be innovative in nature, leveraging, for instance, insights from behavioral economics, reputation management, data science, and gamification. We can make policy more data driven and iterate based on what we learn. For example, a new regulation intended to create jobs can have a specific jobs target against which data is collected. If the result is not achieved, regulators should challenge themselves to understand why they missed the metric and adjust the program to meet the goals.

In addition, we should not limit comment and input to those who know their way around the regulatory process. Regular citizens should be encouraged to participate via crowdsourcing platforms. The federal government should tap into the skills and talents of a wide cross-section of citizens for the co-creation of innovative solutions. Open or more targeted calls using digital platforms around specific challenges and policy questions, potentially prize-induced, have proven to incentivize citizens to engage with government in new and meaningful ways. More experimentation with crowdsourcing digital policy formulation is needed. And we should go beyond that to engage Americans to work with government employees in creative ways that introduce them to the challenges government faces in meeting their needs and draw on public input to make programs more effective. We should be able to show the American people that we can apply America's collective creative genius to make the federal government come alive to serve them.

Improve the Relationship Between the Federal Government and the Tech Sector

Relations between the federal government and the tech sector have been at a nadir since the Edward Snowden revelations. As a result, policy makers have not been able to adequately collaborate with the tech community—a dangerous position considering that a larger and larger share of the problems we need to address will require technological know-how and expertise. And a growing amount of the information the government needs in order to understand the world is going to be in the hands of the tech sector and otherwise unavailable to the government. We have a profoundly strong interest in better collaboration between the government and the tech sector.

We need to recognize that the government, tech sector, and the American public all share the same goal: a healthy, robust, and secure digital economy. Similarly, we ought to appeal to the great patriotism present in the tech sector, begin a new dialogue, and embark on a full-scale redefinition of the federal government's position on issues of importance to the tech sector, such as economic security policy. And we need to embark on collaborative thinking on policy issues that involve the public interest broadly in arenas like artificial intelligence and the Internet of things, and its relationship to privacy generally as the Internet evolves and grows more important in people's lives.

It is not enough for policy makers to turn to the private sector for collaboration or information, or even to have tech experts in government who are at the table. Today, policy makers have to become more tech literate themselves. In a larger sense, technology needs to become a *common* language throughout the federal government. In an earlier period, it was expected that all national security officials, regardless of their background or purview, had an understanding of Cold War geopolitics. While not everyone can know every technology, policy makers can learn about digital technology and have a context for the key issues facing the country.

As in the private sector, our concept of digital technology must shift from being viewed as a tool for economic growth to being seen as the very *foundation* upon which our economy will grow and in which national security decisions will be made.

Conclusion

The global digital economy is racing ahead, and our next president faces a historic choice: either assert a clarion call of leadership or miss the moment to impress upon the nation the importance of adapting to this new era. Other countries have robust national digital economy strategies. Our nation seeks major change, and the next president can set in motion a transformative initiative to expand digital economy jobs and dramatically reshape how the government operates. America led in building the foundation for this tremendous growth; let's not cede leadership now.

Zoë Baird is CEO and President of the Markle Foundation, which focuses on realizing the potential of information technology to address challenging issues in national security, health care, and the economy. She currently leads Rework America, a Markle initiative of more than 50 diverse national leaders focused on creating more paths to opportunity for all Americans in the digital economy. She wrote the preface to the group's collectively authored book, *America's Moment: Creating Opportunity in the Connected Age*, and is leading a national partnership to create a skills-based labor market, Skillful.com. Ms. Baird previously led Markle's efforts to reform the intelligence community and convened The Markle Task Force on National Security in the Information Age. The Task Force reports reframed the role of intelligence in protecting the nation while preserving civil liberties. Ms. Baird also spearheaded Markle's efforts to catalyze improvements in health care, helping drive changes that enabled information to be shared securely and privately. Prior to Markle, she served as Senior Vice President and General Counsel at Aetna; Counselor and Staff Executive at GE; partner at O'Melveny & Myers; Associate Counsel to President Carter; and as Attorney-Advisor at the U.S. Department of Justice. Ms. Baird is founding co-chair of the U.S. Commerce Department's Digital Economy Board of Advisors, a director of the Council on Foreign Relations, an Honorary Trustee of the Brookings Institution, and a member of the Defense Policy Board. Ms. Baird holds an A.B. Phi Beta Kappa and a J.D. from the University of California, Berkeley. She is a member of the Aspen Strategy Group.

[1] See Pew Research Center. November 23, 2015. "Public Trust in Government: 1958-2015." http://www.people-press.org/2015/11/23/public-trust-in-government-1958-2015/

[2] The initiative could be led by the National Security Council, National Economic Council, Office of Science and Technology Policy, Office of Management and Budget, or a special assistant to the president.

[3] See Manyika, James, Sree Ramaswamy, Somesh Khanna, Hugo Sarrazin, Gary Pinkus, Guru Sethupathy, and Andrew Yaffe. December 2015. "Digital America: A Tale of the Haves and Have-Mores." McKinsey Global Institute. http://www.mckinsey.com/industries/high-tech/our-insights/digital-america-a-tale-of-the-haves-and-have-mores/

[4] See Boston Consulting Group. 2016. "The Internet Economy in the G-20." https://www.bcg.com/documents/file100409.pdf

[5] See http://www.sbecouncil.org/about-us/facts-and-data/.

[6] See Baird, Zoë. January 14, 2016. "Dangerous Digital Divide Looming for Small Businesses." *The Hill.* http://thehill.com/blogs/congress-blog/economy-budget/265787-dangerous-digital-divide-looming-for-small-businesses

[7] See *Ebay 2015 US Small Business Global Growth* Report, http://www.ebaymainstreet.com/sites/default/files/2015-us-small-biz-global-growth-report_0.pdf.

[8] See Baird, Zoë and Parker, Emily. May 29, 2015. "A Surprising New Source of American Jobs: China." *Wall Street Journal.* http://www.wsj.com/articles/a-surprising-new-source-of-american-jobs-china-1432922899

[9] See Pew Research Center. 2016. "The State of American Jobs." The data used in this report were based upon both a national public opinion poll and a Pew Research Center analysis of O*NET and Current Population Surveys by the Bureau of Labor Statistics from 1980 to 2015. http://www.pewsocialtrends.org/2016/10/06/the-state-of-american-jobs/

[10] Ryan, Camille L., and Kurt Bauman. March 2016. *Educational Attainment in the United States: 2015.* Washington, DC: U.S. Census Bureau. http://www.census.gov/content/dam/Census/library/publications/2016/demo/p20-578.pdf

"The very technologies that will put public safety at greatest risk will be coupled tightly to U.S. competitiveness in the global economy."

—CHRISTOPHER KIRCHHOFF

Reshaping National Security Institutions for Emerging Technology

Christopher Kirchhoff
Partner
Defense Innovation Unit X
U.S. Department of Defense

As the adage "guns, germs, and steel" calls to mind, technology has long been a driver of power and security. Yet technology is becoming an even more pronounced determinant of the strategic environment today because of the scale at which innovation is happening globally. Greater numbers of scientists and engineers in the U.S. and around the world, backed by new forms of capital, open innovation communities, and the power of the Internet, are developing transformational technologies in new ways. Even high school students in "makers labs"—the shop class of the twenty-first century—are harnessing the revolution in low-cost microelectronics and additive manufacturing to build and invent things that previously required the resources of a research institution.

While this ecosystem of innovation fuels boundless opportunity, it also has a dark side. The diffusion of technology in commercial markets and through the Internet is driving a democratization of destructive and destabilizing capability on a scale never before seen, altering the balance of power globally and between individuals and the state. This historic shift in the means of science and technology production has profound implications for the institutions of U.S. national and homeland security. It also makes policy making in them far more difficult. Encryption, blockchain—the technology that powers the digital currency Bitcoin—autonomous robotics, artificial intelligence, and the widespread availability of genomic editing are among many technologies the next U.S. administration will find vexing precisely because making policy for them requires complex trade-offs between security, economic competitiveness, privacy, and safety. The very technologies that will put public safety at greatest risk will be coupled tightly to U.S. competitiveness in the global economy.

These new technologies present a step-increase in the innovation economy. Homeland and national security agencies are not well equipped to grapple with this intensification. Nor are the interagency policy processes that tie agencies together and to the White House. Yet with modest changes, the nation can substantially grow its capacity to mitigate the risks of emerging technology while taking advantage of the opportunities they offer. In particular, six reforms will prepare the national security apparatus for technology-driven shifts in the strategic environment:

1. Upgrading how departments and agencies make strategic assessments.

2. Bringing "tech teammates" to the policy table.

3. Standing up procurement systems tailor built for the innovation economy.

4. Instantiating internal cultures of innovation and agility.

5. Using digital collaboration tools to mobilize the scope of expertise now necessary for policy making.

6. Positioning the White House to lead on issues of technology by altering the National Security Council's (NSC) structure and deepening its integration with the White House Office of Science and Technology Policy.

Anticipating Shifts in the Strategic Environment

The economy is gushing technology fundamentally disruptive to how homeland and national security institutions perform their missions. Many of these technologies undercut, rather than enhance, how the U.S. projects force and maintains sovereignty over its citizens. To cite a few examples: hobbyists are mounting firearms and explosives to consumer drones. For $12,995, the Austin, Texas-based firm Tracking Point sells a computerized riflescope that enables novice shooters to reliably deliver rounds on target a mile away. 3D manufacturing blueprints for magnetometer-evading handguns are available on the Internet. Perhaps most concerning of all is the lowering cost of genetic-editing tools. The gene-editing technology "CRISPR"—short for clustered regularly interspaced short palindromic repeats—places the ability to cheaply and easily modify the genome of living organisms in the hands of anyone with rudimentary laboratory infrastructure, raising the specter of a "garage" biologist or virologist someday being able to threaten global security. The biosecurity expert Richard Danzig is fond of asking the hypothetical question of what might happen if the Unabomber of tomorrow is a microbiologist rather than a mathematician.

On the higher end of the threat spectrum, technologies are coming online that place capabilities once held by superpowers in the hands of many more militaries, non-state actors, and individuals. The start-up Spire is launching a constellation of microsatellites offering signals intelligence services. Seven other Silicon Valley firms are lobbing microsatellites into space that offer the ability to gaze permanently over wide areas of the earth or zoom in on specific points of interest, with high-resolution imagery delivered in minutes to anyone with a credit card and website access. In a measure of how available the building blocks of key weapons systems are, 96 percent of the components in the U.S. military's most advanced electronic warfare systems are available today on the global microelectronics market.

These are only a few of the technologies and trends that will change what threats Americans face and how the U.S. military and law enforcement organize to protect against them. It takes careful thinking to imagine how they will transform our strategic environment and impact the mission spaces of departments and agencies. It will also require visionary leadership to adapt institutions before sudden shifts in the environment bring about mission failure. Both are needed in greater measure across the national security apparatus.

The first necessary upgrade is one of assessment. While a legion of analysts in the intelligence community track the development of enemy weapons systems with great diligence, only a handful focus on the security implications of commercial technology. Similarly, technical staffs in departments and agencies with the deepest understanding of disruptive technology often sit furthest away from the policy planning staffs that inform decision making. As a result, technology is often an undertheorized factor when analysts evaluate policy courses of action, construct alternate futures, and help senior leaders make pivotal, path-dependent decisions about what risks to buy down and capabilities to acquire.

A few departments have found ways to place technological change more centrally in focus. The best known of these efforts is the Defense Department's Office of Net Assessment. Two generations ago, its analysts accurately forecast how networked sensors would underwrite an era of American dominance in war fighting in which U.S. precision-targeting capabilities far outmatched those of adversaries. That same office then correctly forecast the gradual erosion of U.S. battlefield overmatch, as adversaries mastered this same technology as it diffused onto the global marketplace. The kind of exquisite analysis Net Assessment performs, in which an analyst may spend two years or more working on a single topic in order to chart the strategic choices it presents, has proven invaluable to sixteen secretaries of defense. The FBI also has technology assessment groups in which cross-functional teams of experts explore how bad actors might use new technologies alone or in combination.

These two units showcase the benefits of tying technology-literate strategic assessment tightly into policy planning. Their function deserves to be widely replicated so that decision makers across the national security apparatus can anticipate technologically driven shifts in their mission environment. While the intelligence community, Department of Defense (DoD), and FBI have mature, technology-literate strategic assessment organizations, State Department, Department of Energy, Department of Homeland Security (DHS), Department of Justice, Department of Treasury, Department of Commerce, and U.S. Agency for International Development (USAID) do not.

Embracing "Tech Teammates"

A second ingredient in enhancing the capability of agencies to grapple with emerging technology are technologically literate staff at every level—a literacy often absent, especially at the top of the U.S. government. While national security policy makers regularly integrate lawyers and economists at senior levels, technologists and scientists are often left to make an occasional appearance from their offices down the hall rather than being regular participants in the kitchen cabinets of Cabinet members. This is a curious arrangement given how core science and technology are to problem solving today. Technology is so embedded in policy issues that U.S. Chief Technology Officer Megan Smith is fond of noting that "you need a technologist at the table to know when you need a technologist at the table." Smith, who joined the Obama administration from Google X—Google's moonshot division—uses the apt phrase "tech teammate" to describe the power that comes from adding a technologist to the policy team. She advocates for bringing in tech teammates who have worked with technology at scale in industry for short one- to three-year "term tours" and then allowing them to return to the private sector. Commercial technology is advancing so rapidly that anyone who has been in government more than a few years is by definition out-of-date.

The way to increase the flow of tech teammates into the national security apparatus is to build "on-ramps" through flexible and term hiring mechanisms as well as "off-ramps" for government personnel to take industry sabbaticals and externships. Top technologists must be actively recruited away from compelling private sector opportunities rather than relying on an obscure posting on USAJobs.gov to attract the right candidate. Equally important, the government must change over time the incentive structure of technology professionals in industry and academia to encourage the same kind of term tours in government for which lawyers and economists are rewarded. If successful in recruiting tech teammates, the next administration can create a "thin layer" of technical expertise, tightly coupled to industry, that constitutes a government-wide community of practice in emerging technology.

The Obama administration has already shown this is possible. The Presidential Innovation Fellows program, created by the White House Office of Science and Technology Policy in 2012 and formalized by Executive Order in 2016, recruits performers from the top 1 percent of the tech industry into government service. Most of these fellows take enormous salary cuts—think subtracting a zero—for the chance to serve one- to three-year tours in Washington before returning to the private sector. While to date Presidential Innovation Fellows have mostly consisted of coders and product managers working to improve citizen-facing digital services, in summer 2016, the administration created a national and homeland security track within the program. The track opens a promising on-ramp for a broader range of tech talent to work on applied problems in national and homeland security. The program aspires for its candidates to receive expedited top secret/sensitive compartmented information clearances and to seat them just a few months after their selection. While the first class of national and homeland security Presidential Innovation Fellows is small, it includes two former CEOs of major technology companies and experts in robotics, blockchain technology, cybersecurity, and venture capital. This effort joins Secretary of Defense Ash Carter's Force of the Future initiative as well as newly announced cyber hiring authorities and other excepted service mechanisms, which the Office of Personnel Management is devolving to agencies to help address the pressing need to bring tech teammates to the policy table.

Accessing the Innovation Economy

In addition to tech teammates, far faster access to technology is needed. To achieve this, acquisition practices need to be retuned to the rhythms of the innovation economy. Over the past two generations, the federal government has gone from a "net exporter" of advanced technology to a "net importer" of software, hardware, and services. It's not just that the commercial technology sector funds innovative research and development at a rate more than double that of federal R&D, with, for example, Google and Apple having more than twice the market capitalization of General Dynamics, Northrop Grumman, Lockheed Martin, and Raytheon combined. Innovation is now occurring in many decentralized start-ups that are hard to identify and harder still to do business with using traditional procurement mechanisms.

The cumulative effects of these trends are striking. Government procurement remains mostly optimized for buying from large companies with federal sales divisions able to navigate the requirements processes, federal acquisition rules, and separate accounting regimes mandated by the Defense Contract Audit Agency. It doesn't take an MBA to grasp that federal sales are only a fraction of the $25 trillion global consumer market and for that reason do not merit mention in the business plan of most start-ups. Pursuing this sliver of the overall market is even less attractive to young companies because they must wait months or years for a contract to come to fruition when investors, to justify further rounds of capital infusion, want to see results in days and weeks. The way federal agencies buy technology acts as a moat separating the federal castle from the emerging technology kingdom it presides over. As a result, the government is structurally shut out of many of the most promising technologies until the firms that produce them go public and build the machinery to sell to the public sector. The end result is a five- to seven-year lag before the government can initiate the lengthy process of procuring technology that commercial firms have been using for years.

To overcome this impedance mismatch and the cumulative lag it imposes, ten federal agencies are setting up satellite offices in Silicon Valley. Some of them couple rapid acquisition methods with teams of technology scouts. Others are "points of presence" aimed at facilitating interaction but not technology ingestion. In-Q-Tel, the intelligence community's strategic investment firm, has been active for over a decade. It is now joined by DoD's newly rebooted Defense Innovation Unit X (DIUx) and outfits from DHS, the General Services Administration (GSA), Commerce, the Patent Office, FBI, State, and USAID.

The irony is that most national and homeland security agencies already have the authorities they need to engage with technology firms on commercial terms. "Other contracting authority," or OTA, is a federal authority that is the brainchild of former General Counsel of the Defense Advanced Research Projects Agency (DARPA) Rick Dunn. OTAs are specifically designed for technology experimentation, sit outside the federal acquisition rules (FAR), and cannot be protested. DIUx has fashioned a new type of OTA called a commercial solutions opening that boasts many new features. It allows DIUx to post simple descriptions of problems on its website. Firms tender solutions by sending in the same pitch deck they show venture capital firms. If DIUx wants to move ahead, funding can be executed within 30 days of proposal receipt. DIUx also takes advantage of a "contracting superpower" granted to DoD by Congress in the 2016 National Defense Authorization Act. This new authority allows the

OTA merit-based selection process to constitute justification for subsequent follow-on sole-source production awards under either an OTA or FAR-based contract. A military end-customer who likes the technology piloted under an OTA can immediately transition into a program of record, smoothing the path through the infamous "valley of death."

Institutional Innovation

Just as buying technology quickly is essential in a future filled with strategic surprise, organizational agility within the national security apparatus is also crucial. There are at least three components of agility relevant to emerging technology. First, the presence of advanced technology organs, like DARPA and the Intelligence Advanced Research Projects Activity (IARPA), which help prevent strategic surprise by experimenting with the very technology likely to cause it. Second, the embedding of technical talent at every layer in the organization, and most crucially on the leadership team, in a role separate and distinct from a chief information officer (i.e., a chief technology officer or chief innovation officer focused on technology adoption writ large rather than managing enterprise IT systems). Third, internal innovation accelerators and innovation marketplaces, often crowdsourced and crowd-funded, that enable employees to experiment on smaller scales with solutions they devise and then institutionalize when successful. These three components allow innovation to drift in from the side, brew from the bottom up, and be called for from the top.

USAID has developed a compelling way to wrap together all of these qualities. Its Global Development Lab, an advanced technology organ not unlike DARPA, established an "Operational Innovation Team" focused solely on innovating business practices that support technology experimentation. Its members are drawn from the main USAID offices for human resources, general counsel, information systems, and procurement. Their charge is to find a "path to yes" for specific project teams within the Lab. They then have the mandate to help all of USAID adopt approaches that prove successful. Already, the Operational Innovation Team has succeeded in mainlining novel rapid procurement practices, tour-of-duty hiring, and active recruiting. The National Security Agency's Incubation Cell and Spark, an intelligence community-wide crowdsourced innovation platform, is another example of how agencies can create in themselves the agility they need to respond to shifts in the strategic environment.

Interagency Collaboration and NSC Process

The final reform needed to deal with emerging technology has to do with the policy process that ties the national security apparatus together. While the U.S. government boasts an impressive command-and-control system that enables senior leaders to conference with each other and the president 24/7, this system has surprising shortcomings. The same set of leaders who can be put into a videoconference with the president in minutes are not able to edit a shared document in real time, build a wiki together, or even open a chat window. These basic digital collaboration tools are regularly used even by elementary school children and across the private sector. While some national security workers do have some of these collaboration tools, they often cannot be used for cross-agency collaboration or with others outside government. This "productivity tax" hinders the interchange between agencies that is necessary as policy makers confront issues that cut across the missions of multiple agencies. National security agencies should also take full advantage of natural language processing to enable textual search and automatic knowledge management of large bodies of documents. It should not be the case that law firms have a suite of discovery tools that far surpass those used by a foreign service officer or a defense policy analyst.

The very fact that emerging technology typically has security, regulatory, and commercial implications also makes White House leadership on technology policy crucial. The next administration will not be able to rely on any one department to lead the U.S. response to most emerging technologies. The NSC's convening role on technology issues is therefore vital. In order to play that role as effectively as possible, the NSC will need greater internal capacity as well as tighter integration with the White House Office of Science and Technology Policy. The incoming administration will have an opportunity to consider alternative organization models that may be more robust and sustainable over the long term.

Presently, most technology policy issues fall to the NSC directorates of Cyber, Defense, WMD, or Resilience. None are necessarily staffed with the expertise to handle deeply technical matters. These directorates must also uncomfortably balance staffing their primary responsibilities with ad hoc tech policy issues assigned to them for resolution. Creating a dedicated Technology Policy Directorate within the NSC is an obvious organizational adjustment. Its workload could include the highly technical issues now being handled by other directorates as well as spearheading deeper integration with the White House Office of Science and Technology Policy, whose new

Office of the U.S. Chief Technology Officer and Technology Policy Task Force are wading heavily into matters with security implications. A Technology Directorate could also provide a home for the NSC's own in-house tech teammates. The NSC presently has few scientists and engineers within it and even lacks a computer scientist of stature in its Cyber Directorate.

Emerging technology and cybersecurity issues will have such a defining role in the national security space that the incoming administration may even wish to create a deputy assistant to the president-level position overseeing it. This would enable the administration to attract a heavyweight from industry able to convene policy committees at the right levels within the White House and across government. Creating such a position would also send an unmistakable signal to industry about the seriousness with which the administration is treating emerging technology, which would in turn foster new openings for collaboration. The NSC's Strategic Planning Directorate should also add a director and senior director focused on technology strategy with the explicit mandate to convene strategic planners from across national and homeland security agencies.

A Brave New World

We are living at a unique moment in the history of technology, where sweeping changes in how innovation happens is enabling invention and discovery on a grand scale. The fruits of this new ecosystem are changing how we live and work, while also posing profound challenges to how we maintain our security. Readying national and homeland security institutions for this brave new world will take dogged leadership. The steps that must be taken cut across the grain of existing practices. The hiring system is brittle and overseen by a federal office that styles itself as the upholder of the civil service system, which was originally devised in the era of the telegraph to staff the post office. A strong cultural bias toward requirements-based contracting is deeply rooted in the acquisition community. Even the NSC has yet to invite to its weekly staff meetings a representative from the Office of the U.S. Chief Technology Officer, whose personnel include several of the world's experts on encryption, cybersecurity, and autonomous technology.

Yet steps must be taken. Leaving these trends unaddressed risks mission failure on an unthinkable scale.

Christopher Kirchhoff is one of four partners overseeing the Pentagon's Silicon Valley Office, Defense Innovation Unit X, and its nation-wide investment portfolio harnessing emerging commercial technology for national security innovation. Previously, he was Director for Strategic Planning at the National Security Council and Special Assistant to General Martin E. Dempsey, the Chairman of the Joint Chiefs of Staff. Dr. Kirchhoff also served in the White House Chief of Staff's office as Senior Advisor to Presidential Counselor John Podesta, under whom he authored the White House report on Big Data & Privacy. He has been awarded the Secretary of Defense Medal for Outstanding Public Service and the Civilian Service Medal for hazardous duty in Iraq. From 2011-2014, he was the highest ranking openly gay advisor in the U.S. military. Dr. Kirchhoff graduated with highest honors in History and Science from Harvard College and holds a doctorate in politics from Cambridge University, where he was a Gates Scholar.

Part 3

THE MACHINERY OF THE U.S. GOVERNMENT

"Because the current administration and past administrations haven't dedicated sufficient time to thinking through any significant structural challenges to the NSC, the capable professionals that work there find themselves battling a tumultuous international landscape with a system and toolkit that are sorely outdated."

—JULIANNE SMITH

Reforming the National Security Council:
Three Questions for the Next President

Julianne Smith
Senior Fellow
Director, Strategy and Statecraft Program
Center for a New American Security (CNAS)

During the nearly three months between the U.S. presidential election on November 8th and Inauguration Day on January 20th, transition teams across U.S. government agencies will undertake the arduous task of reviewing current policies, outlining prospective personnel changes, and identifying policy and structural changes the next president should make once he or she arrives in the Oval Office. Traditionally, the transition teams focus more on policy than process. That could change this year given the ongoing debates that Congress, Washington think tanks, and former senior Obama administration officials are having about the National Security Council (NSC).

The roots of those debates stem largely from one fundamental critique: the NSC has become both too big and too domineering, inserting itself into the daily business of the State and Defense Departments. But in many ways, arguing over the exact size of the NSC misses the point. The world has changed dramatically since the NSC was created in 1947, and, yet, only modest changes have been made to the NSC throughout a number of past administrations. The end result is that the U.S. government continues to rely on a national security system that is ill-equipped to cope with today's fast-paced, fluid, and dangerous global landscape. This paper argues that if the next president wants to ensure that the national security system is as resilient, innovative, and agile as possible, he or she must answer three fundamental questions about the future of the NSC: What is the NSC's primary mission? What accompanying structure best fits that mission? And, how can the NSC build in strategic pauses?

An Outdated System for New Challenges

Today's security environment simply has no precedent. No single challenge to U.S. interests is equivalent to those posed by Nazi Germany, imperial Japan, or the Soviet Union during the twentieth century. Instead, the United States faces an interconnected web of global and regional threats, whose sheer volume and complexity are overwhelming. A broad array of actors, ranging from great powers to rogue states to non-state actors, are turning to an increasingly sophisticated and ever-evolving set of tactics. Whether it is Russia's use of hybrid warfare or China's reliance on anti-access, area denial (A2/AD) capabilities or Islamic extremists' attacks on soft targets, America's adversaries are constantly finding new and creative ways to challenge U.S. interests and undermine U.S. comparative advantages.

At the same time, America's relationship with the world has evolved in significant ways. On the one hand, U.S. leadership is being challenged by countries intent on increasing their own influence in their neighborhood or within regional alliances. It is therefore not as easy for the United States to shape outcomes and influence world events, especially inside the many international institutions that the U.S. helped create. On the other hand, many of those same countries that consistently challenge U.S. leadership continue to turn to the United States to solve global crises like the Ebola outbreak or the rise of the Islamic State. Washington thus finds itself navigating two broad trends: an evolving international security system rich with emerging powers intent on redefining it, and a near constant demand for the United States to lead the response to every global challenge.

Both the current and past administrations have done their best to adjust to these realities. But change has largely come in the form of new policies and new policy tools (i.e., economic statecraft, building partnership capacity, or a new cyber command). Less has been done to alter the structure and mechanics of the NSC. To be sure, every president enters office with a different "command climate," which sets the tone, style, and pace of day-to-day operations and alters the ways in which the NSC operates. Presidents also tend to add or remove various subject matter NSC directorates or offices, enabling them to place special emphasis on a particular region or functional issue. President George W. Bush, for example, significantly increased the NSC's work on counter-terrorism in the wake of the September 11 attacks, for all the obvious reasons. President Obama put added emphasis on arms control when he arrived in office, altering the size and structure of that particular office inside the NSC.

While modifying directorates inside the NSC is an important way for a president to shape the work of the NSC, those types of changes have failed to get at the heart of the challenge. The Project for National Security Reform (PNSR), from 2008, perhaps said it best when it concluded that "The legacy structures and processes of a national security system that is now more than 60 years old no longer help American leaders to formulate coherent national strategy."[1] Because the current administration and past administrations haven't dedicated sufficient time to thinking through any significant structural challenges to the NSC, the capable professionals that work there find themselves battling a tumultuous international landscape with a system and toolkit that are sorely outdated. Today, NSC staff describe a system that leaves them lurching from one crisis to another, is too reactive, provides little to no time to think strategically, and has evolved into a crisis management shop.

Three Questions About the Next Administration's National Security Council

To ensure that the U.S. national security system is best positioned to address today's rapidly changing global security environment and that the professionals that start work at the NSC in early 2017 begin their tenure with the strongest, most efficient system possible, the next president needs to answer three core questions *before* entering office.

What is the NSC's primary mission?

The NSC was designed in the late 1940s to do two things: drive presidential decision making and ensure that those decisions are implemented across the U.S. government. Over the years, that mission has evolved and expanded, leaving the NSC staff grappling with an array of competing and overlapping priorities. NSC staff continue to tee up decisions for the president and his cabinet, but they also often manage global crises, formulate policy, formulate strategy, manage how agencies implement policy, and staff the president and vice president in advance of and during trips abroad and in high-level foreign engagements at home. And they do all this while attending a dizzying array of interagency meetings that cover too many issues in too much detail.

The NSC has been repeatedly criticized for being too large, with today's number hovering just under 400 staff—the largest in U.S. history.[2] (The number of professional staff is closer to 200, though.) As NSC staff have come to realize, though, 400 individuals are still too few to undertake the multiple mission sets listed above. Everyone agrees, though, that adding more staff isn't the answer. In fact, many assume that increasing the size of the NSC staff would likely make today's challenges much worse. And even if the next president wanted to increase the size of the NSC staff, the White House lacks a place to put them, as the Executive Office Building, where NSC staff work, is already at peak capacity. Those realities leave the next president with one choice: design a more limited role for the NSC and return some of the NSC's current functions to other agencies.

Obviously, making the NSC less operational will involve trade-offs. The White House may have to accept somewhat less control as it places increased trust in the heads of other agencies to take the lead on messaging and formulating and implementing policy. But freeing the NSC staff of some of the burden of tracking every policy-related detail will help it maintain strategic focus on both the president's top priorities and the most pressing challenges. The next president should therefore do his or her best—well in advance of arriving in the Oval Office—to establish clear guidance on when the NSC should lead and when it should empower other U.S. agencies, like the State Department and the Defense Department. And when, not if, that arrangement inevitably breaks down and the White House finds that an agency is failing to meet expectations or heading in an unexpected direction, the president and his advisors must resist the temptation to shift control back to the White House. Instead, changes should be made at the agency in question, even if change means removing and replacing a member of the president's cabinet. Too often White House frustration with other agencies results in the conclusion that the White House needs to take control, which in turn fuels White House micromanagement.[3]

What accompanying structure best fits the NSC mission?

Once the president provides clarity on the NSC mission, several structural decisions will need to stem from that. Such decisions can be divided into two broad categories: organizational and process. In terms of organization, the next president must decide if he or she wants to make changes to the current configuration of directorates inside the NSC beyond enlarging one or two of them to reflect policy priorities. Does, for example, the White House need a separate NSC directorate, each with five to ten staff members, for every region and functional issue? Are there better ways to tackle the cross-cutting nature of today's complex security environment? Could regional and functional experts sit together, perhaps in task forces, to address issues that cross their respective areas of expertise? Should other models be considered? Irrespective of what the next president decides, his or her decision must be made early, as structural changes are tough to make years into a president's term.[4]

Important staffing questions are also part of the organizational decisions the next president will need to make. President Obama and President Bush both experimented with the appointment of "czars" or special coordinators to take the lead on issues of the utmost importance. Bush, for example, created a "war czar" that had the rank of assistant to the president and reported directly to the president on the ongoing wars in both Iraq and Afghanistan. Those types of positions bring multiple advantages, particularly for national security advisors that lack the time to manage a new policy decision or strategy for months or even years on end. Putting a single person in charge to drive and chair interagency meetings, keep the president informed, and ensure that the wheels of the bureaucracy keep turning in all the right directions can produce real dividends. But these positions also create internal friction and confusion, especially within the NSC and across the interagency since they add another layer to the institutional hierarchy. The next president should thus be cautious about applying this model. To the extent that he or she feels a special czar is needed, the president should ensure the number of czars doesn't unnecessarily proliferate. Ideally, there should only be one, maybe two, such individuals on staff, and it will be important for the president to provide clarity on that person's role and authorities.

In addition to structure, questions of process are equally important to consider, particularly as they relate to the pace of high-level interagency meetings. For some time now, the chairs of mid-level interagency meetings at the assistant secretary and deputy assistant secretary levels have been accused of pushing too many decisions to deputies and principals. To be sure, seemingly minor decisions sometimes require principal-level attention simply because they involve trade-offs that can only be properly adjudicated at a higher level. For example, assistant secretaries and their deputies are typically responsible for individual regional or functional areas, and thus are not well suited to—or held accountable for—adjudicating issues that allocate resources *globally* in ways that effectively balance competing strategic priorities. But in recent years, interagency staff members have complained that far too many decisions are being pushed to deputies and principals, filling their days with hours of meetings in the Situation Room and detracting from the time they have to manage the business of running their own agencies. When Susan Rice became President Obama's national security advisor in 2013, she conducted a thorough review of the NSC and concluded that the number of deputy committee meetings (DCs) should be reduced, freeing those high-level officials to spend more time at their home agencies. The next president and his or her national security advisor should follow suit and identify other ways the NSC can push decision making down to lower levels of government.

How can the NSC build in strategic pauses?

Finally, given the complex nature of today's national security environment, the president should work with his national security team to identify four or five ways he or she might build in strategic pauses that force the staff to occasionally step away from the tactical decisions that need to be made within hours. The current national security advisor, Susan Rice, has made some important changes in this regard. The NSC now holds regular DCs on long-term trends, which have been applauded and are well-attended. Similarly, the State Department has created its own Strategy Lab designed to create a space inside the building that is free of the usual operational demands and pressures one encounters in the bureaucracy. The next president should build on these initiatives but go beyond them. More specifically, he or she should consider:

- Creating a Strategic Foresight Cell inside the NSC that can conduct tabletop exercises. That cell could also "red team" U.S. policies by asking officials to view a problem through the eyes of U.S. competitors in order to revisit their original assumptions and objectives, ask hard questions, and look beyond short-term requirements.

- Conducting an Annual Strategy Review to evaluate the most recent strategy documents (National Security Strategy, National Military Strategy, Quadrennial Diplomacy and Development Review, and Quadrennial Defense Review) against current events. What have they gotten wrong? Where should the administration make midcourse corrections?

- Assessing risk with allies. The United States regularly works with partners and allies to address global crises, but the NSC should also develop ways to work with them to assess risks before crises erupt. None of the existing international organizations perform this role. The next president may want to consider creating a forum that would identify emerging threats, conduct risk assessments, and host tabletop scenarios with allies to highlight policy gaps.[5] No one can predict the future, particularly in today's uncertain security landscape, but that is precisely why conducting risk assessments is so important.

In many ways, the messy business of policy making is unavoidable, especially in the NSC. Unanticipated world events will continue to test even the best national security systems. And social media will continue to put unprecedented pressure on administrations to respond in real time. Personality conflicts, turf battles, stress, and long hours will also remain a key feature of the NSC and the interagency in general. But utilizing the transition period to focus on the more tedious questions of process and structure will maximize the next president's chances of realizing his or her strategic policy goals.

Julianne Smith is Senior Fellow and Director of the Strategy and Statecraft Program at the Center for a New American Security. Ms. Smith also serves as a Senior Advisor to Beacon Global Strategies. Earlier, she served as Deputy National Security Advisor to Vice President Biden from April 2012 to June 2013. During March and April of 2013, she served as Acting National Security Advisor to the Vice President. Prior to the White House, she served as Principal Director for European and NATO Policy in the Office of the Secretary of Defense, acting as the principal staff assistant and advisor to the Assistant Secretary of Defense for International Security Affairs. Before joining the Obama administration, Ms. Smith served as director of the CSIS Europe Program. Earlier, she worked at the German Marshall Fund as program officer for the Foreign Policy Program and director of communications for the Project on the Role of American Military Power. She was a senior analyst on the European security desk of the British American Security Information Council and in Germany at the Stiftung Wissenschaft und Politik as a Robert Bosch Foundation Fellow. Ms. Smith is a recipient of the American Academy in Berlin Public Policy Fellowship and the Fredin Memorial Scholarship for study at the Sorbonne. She received her B.A. from Xavier University and her M.A. from American University.

---

[1] Project on National Security Reform. November 2008. *Forging a New Shield*. Washington, DC: Center for the Study of the Presidency. http://0183896.netsolhost.com/site/wp-content/uploads/2011/12/pnsr_forging_a_new_shield_report.pdf

[2] Part of the growth under the Obama administration stems from the merger of the Homeland Security Council with the National Security Council.

[3] Of course, as Derek Chollet pointed out in his September 8, 2016, testimony on the House Committee on Foreign Affairs, some amount of bureaucratic overreach is unavoidable, particularly since "the President will be the one held accountable by the public, press, the Congress, and the American people."

[4] One exception to that is the effort pursued by President Obama's current national security advisor, Susan Rice, who conducted a full review of the National Security Council on arrival and launched a reform effort fairly late into the president's second term.

[5] Smith, Julianne. 2016. "Our Overworked Security Bureaucracy." *Democracy: A Journal of Ideas* 40 (Spring). http://democracyjournal.org/author/julianne-smith/

"It is the case that a president gets the NSC system that the president deserves. It is the president's vehicle, and the president's responsibility."

—STEPHEN HADLEY

Reforming the National Security Council:
Policy Prescriptions and Recommendations

Stephen Hadley
Former National Security Advisor
to President George W. Bush

The current National Security Council (NSC) system simply cannot cope with the vast array of national security, homeland security, and foreign, defense, and economic policy challenges that the United States faces in the world today. The current centralized structure of a hierarchy of interagency committees, culminating in the Deputies Committee, Principals Committee, and the National Security Council itself, is basically unchanged from what Henry Kissinger established as national security advisor (NSA) under President Nixon in the 1960s.

The bandwidth of that system is too limited to cope with today's wide range of challenges. Under the current system, by the time an issue gets to the point of receiving high-level attention, it is usually fairly late in the evolution of the issue and often to the point of crisis. At that moment, the soft-power options (diplomacy, security assistance, economic sanctions, etc.) are in the rearview mirror—because there is insufficient time for them to have any real effect on the current crisis. This means that too often the president is left with a choice that boils down either to using military force or doing nothing. If issues continually need to get to the crisis point before they get high-level attention, as often occurs in the current system, then an administration is likely to deal only with more crises—because it will not have had the time to put in place strategies and policies designed to shape events in ways congenial to American interests and to avoid crises.

In addition, the current system has tended to absorb into the interagency process too many issues in too much detail. The "process" has over several administrations evolved to the point where it is "grinding too small"—involving deputies, principals, and even the president too far into the details of a policy and too far away from overall questions of context, objectives, and strategy. There are now too many interagency meetings at senior levels, which detract from the time that NSC principals in particular need to manage and lead their respective departments and agencies.

Technology has not helped. The capability to use secure video links to bring virtually into the Situation Room ambassadors and military commanders from within the relevant theater is a terrific tool for crisis management. But when it is used as well for more routine policy discussions, it invites senior Washington policy officials to get too far into the "weedy" details and tactics of an issue—and, again, away from a discussion of overall context, objectives, and strategy. Too many interagency meetings scheduled to last 50 minutes start out by diving deeply into the details of a particular policy issue—and only after 40 minutes or so does someone have the temerity to say: "Wait a minute. What are we trying to do here?" That is where any meeting of senior policy officials should begin, not end. The press of routine business plus the plethora of interagency meetings leaves senior policy officials with too little time to think.

In his book *Issues On My Mind,* former Secretary of State George Shultz relates that at least once a week he would tell his front office staff that he was going to go into his office, close the door, and was not to be disturbed for the next hour or so—unless he was called either by his wife or by the president, in that order (showing the priority he placed on domestic affairs over foreign policy!). He would then go into his office, take pencil and paper, and begin to think about the issue of the moment—and write down what the United States was trying to do, and how it should try to do it.

It is likely the case that no senior official observes this practice today. Yet it is essential if senior officials are to be in a position to give the president thoughtful and cogent advice—and if an administration is to get ahead of crises, rather than simply react to them. The other problem is staying focused on priorities and not being distracted by secondary issues.

Former Secretary of State Condoleezza Rice used to keep on her desk a list of four or five items that were her priorities for a given month—and she would return to that list on an almost daily basis, always asking herself whether she was actually making progress on those listed items despite all the other issues vying for her attention.

Successive administrations—from Henry Kissinger's time and forward—have also been relatively unsuccessful in incorporating deliberate forward-looking strategic-level discussion and planning into the interagency process. Creating a small two- to three-person staff within the NSC staff dedicated to such "strategic foresight" is a good first step. The George W. Bush and other administrations also used that strategy staff to lead and coordinate strategic planning among the policy planning staffs of the various departments and agencies.

Another useful tool is the Obama administration's deputies-level "foresight process," resulting in periodic deputies meetings to address longer-term trends. Presentations by the National Intelligence Council and the Central Intelligence Agency tee up these meetings. Among other things, the meetings evaluate existing policies in terms of whether they make sense in light of the overall regional or global context, whether assumptions on which the policy is based have changed, and whether different organizational or implementation approaches are needed.

There is a pretty broad consensus among practitioners and academics in favor of the "Scowcroft Model" for how the NSA plays her or his role. But, there are certain prerequisites if this model is to be effective. They include: a president who makes clear to the NSA and the national security principals that the Scowcroft "honest broker" model is what the president wants; national security, homeland security, and foreign, defense, and economic policy principals (especially the secretaries of state and defense), who are substantial figures in their own right, have strong ties to the president and are willing to insist (to the president if necessary) that the NSA observe the tenets of the Scowcroft Model—as the president has directed; an NSA whose personality, temperament, and operating style fit fairly naturally with the model; and a level of collegiality, transparency, coordination, and trust among the NSC principals, including especially the secretaries of state and defense.

For example, both Tom Donilon and I had a practice of coordinating with the secretary of state if we were meeting with a foreign leader, foreign minister, or even fellow NSA—to ensure that there were no surprises, and that the secretary (as well as the president) were all coordinated on the message we NSAs were going to deliver. Indeed, we found it highly effective if we and the respective secretary of state conducted coordinated, parallel approaches to the foreign minister and NSA of a given country, respectively, using a common message reflecting a common strategy—often, if you will, helping to coordinate the position of foreign governments from the outside in ways congenial to American interests.

Below are a series of policy prescriptions for the new president to address the shortcomings of the NSC and possible measures to reform the existing system.

1. National security is a team sport. Key considerations in developing recommendations regarding the persons to head the eight to ten most important national security, homeland security, and foreign, defense, and economic policy departments and agencies ought to be: whether the persons are known to the president and have the president's trust and confidence; whether the persons are known to each other, have a history of working together successfully, and have each other's trust and confidence; and whether the persons can work together as a team in support of the president and the president's policies.

2. People are as important as process. Good process can improve the prospects that an administration will have sound policies, but people often count for more—they can defeat good process, and they can sometimes produce good results even from bad process. The White House Personnel Office needs to work closely with the NSA (and the deputy NSA) to ensure that persons who are tapped to serve in subcabinet positions in the key national security, homeland security, and foreign, defense, and economic policy departments and agencies have substantive qualifications for those jobs and can work constructively together as part of the president's team. These are not jobs for rookies, first-timers, or prima donnas. This needs to be a team sport at every level of government—and the president needs to insist on it all the way down the chain.

3. Establish an effective national security strategy process. This needs to be established at the very outset of the administration. The character and strength of this process has varied from administration to administration. Its principal product is usually a document setting out the national security strategy for the new administration.

Often these documents are more tactical than strategic, resembling a laundry list of fairly disconnected second-order policies, which get put on the shelf and have little impact on what the new administration actually does in the world. The process needs to be re-engineered to produce a strategic framework for the new administration that will drive its priorities, initiatives, and foreign, defense, security, and economic policies.

The National Defense Panel, co-chaired by Bill Perry and I, reviewed the 2010 Quadrennial Defense Review and recommended such a process; its recommendations are a good place to start. The importance of this process for the new administration is not just the document it produces but that it can force a strategic conversation between the new president and the president's national security, homeland security, and foreign, defense, and economic policy team about the broad strategic direction, priorities, and initiatives of the new administration.

4. Institutionalize strategic thinking and strategic planning. This is essential if the NSC interagency process is to be forward-looking and developing strategies for shaping future events and heading off crises.

As discussed previously, there needs to be a small staff element within the NSC staff tasked with strategic foresight and strategy development and a process by which this staff element can coordinate and lead the strategy and policy planning elements in the departments and agencies. While their work must be operationally relevant, they must be protected from becoming sucked in to day-to-day issues and the crisis of the moment. Perhaps the biggest challenge will be to find a way routinely to bring the output and perspective of this strategic foresight and strategy development process before busy senior-level officials—and a president—too often so overwhelmed by the press of the immediate that they are unable adequately to attend to the important.

5. Establish a Council of Historical Advisers. Graham Allison and Niall Ferguson make this suggestion. The council would be a group of three to five historians serving the president and the NSC.

The purpose of the council would be to bring applied history—and its lessons, precedents, and analogies—to bear on the challenges and opportunities of the present. As Allison and Ferguson have written: "Although applied historians will never be clairvoyants with unclouded crystal balls, we agree with Winston Churchill: 'The longer you can look back, the farther you can look forward.'"

6. Get the interagency process out of the weeds. The purpose of the NSC interagency process should be to set broad policy and then rely on distributed, decentralized execution and implementation by the relevant departments and agencies.

From a policy development perspective, the NSC process needs to be more strategic and less tactical. Its focus should be helping the president, with the advice of the NSC principals (the relevant senior cabinet secretaries and agency heads), to set overall national objectives—and then develop the broad outlines of the strategies required to achieve those objectives.

The NSA and the NSC staff need to be self-limiting with respect to power—and resist the temptation to drive the interagency process down into the tactical details and try to dictate those details. From a policy implementation perspective, the NSA and the NSC staff should oversee and coordinate the development of the execution plans required to carry out those strategies—plans under which the departments and agencies assume execution responsibility for the various elements of strategy within their respective areas of authority and competence.

The NSA and the NSC staff should monitor and oversee department and agency execution of these plans to ensure it is done with the urgency and focus required to achieve the objectives of the president's strategy—and measure the results whenever possible. But actual implementation and execution should be left to the line departments and agencies—and should not be assumed by the NSC staff.

7. Empower and enable your people. The cabinet secretaries and agency heads are the officials that the Senate has confirmed and to whom the Congress and the American people look to carry out American foreign, defense, security, and economic policy. That is not the role of the White House or the NSC staffs—whose members are not Senate confirmed, do not testify before Congress, and should be relatively unknown to the American people.

Distributed, decentralized execution and implementation will require the president to empower and enable the cabinet secretaries and agency heads. But it will also require that the under secretary and assistant secretary levels within those departments and agencies be similarly empowered and enabled—as well as the president's representatives "in the field" (the ambassadors, military commanders, and intelligence officers who represent the arms and legs of the American government abroad).

One way for the president to empower and enable is explicitly to give a cabinet secretary, one of her or his subordinates, or an existing ambassador or military commander the lead in executing a specific policy or initiative—and "dual-hatting" the cabinet secretary or official with a supplemental presidential title (in addition to her or his position in the line organization) as evidence of the fact that she or he carries the authority and confidence of the president in this matter.

Such an approach may not work in every situation—especially where the policy or initiative involves major responsibilities of multiple agencies. In these cases, the president can consider dual-hatting co-leads from the two departments or agencies most involved. (Note, as precedent, the close relationship between U.S. Ambassador to Iraq Ryan Crocker and General David Petraeus, commander of U.S. forces in Iraq, during the "Surge" in 2007-2008.)

In many cases, such dual-hatting will be appropriate—and dual-hatting someone within a line organization or in an existing position avoids all the bureaucratic uncertainties and resistance caused by the appointment of a "presidential envoy" or "policy czar" from outside any existing organization. Having so empowered and enabled them, the president must also hold his cabinet officers and department heads (and their subordinates) accountable—and replace them if they fail to perform. Should an execution problem arise, the president must resist the temptation to pull the issue up into the White House and try to substitute the NSC staff for what is a deficiency in the line organization. Fix the problem at its source—fix the problem in the line organization—and do not try to substitute staff for line.

Encourage your cabinet secretaries and agency heads to work together to develop common approaches to challenges and opportunities. Don't insist that every such initiative come up through the formal NSC interagency process. It is enough if the president and the NSA are kept apprised and able to offer course correction if required.

Secretary of State Rice and Secretary of Defense Gates did this very effectively in the George W. Bush administration, and Secretary Gates and Secretary of State Clinton did it very effectively in the Barack Obama administration. Similarly, the Strategic & Economic Dialogue between the United States and China under the Obama administration (and its predecessor under the George W. Bush administration) were effectively co-chaired on the U.S. side by the secretary of state and the secretary of the treasury. This kind of cabinet-level (and sub-cabinet-level) cooperation can be particularly effective in the field of "economic diplomacy," as discussed later in this chapter.

For this kind of cross-agency integration and cooperation to work, there needs to be—in the words of Jim Steinberg—a "common and effective information-sharing environment" or platform, at both unclassified and classified levels, across all the key departments and agencies involved in the NSC interagency process. And it would be enhanced if there were also a "common assessment" process integrating the various sources of information from both across and outside the government. More broadly: the whole government needs to be on one network—and a network that works.

8. Put all the players on the field. Using a phrase very much in vogue in national security circles, to promote American interests in this challenging world will require "all elements of national power" to be harnessed in the service of common national objectives. This in turn will require the president to take advantage of the full range of contributions, perspectives, and skills that are available both inside and outside of government to address national challenges and opportunities.

Within the federal government, for example, the relevant economic and homeland security departments and agencies are too often not at the NSC table when major national security, homeland security, and foreign, defense, and economic policy issues are discussed. Most recent presidents have invited the secretary of the treasury to attend NSC meetings when monetary or financial issues may be involved (such as economic sanctions). But financial and economic factors are now so integral to American national security and foreign policy that the treasury secretary should be present at virtually every NSC meeting.

a. The secretary of commerce, by contrast, is usually absent from such meetings. This is a mistake that needs to be corrected. The U.S. government often fails to appreciate the influence of the U.S. private sector abroad. As Secretary Pritzker has written, foreign governments want American companies to be operating and investing in their countries because they offer the promise of economic growth, investment, and jobs. "This provides the USG an effective opportunity to influence foreign government decision-making when our objectives align with those of the private sector."

This is particularly the case when a country needs to make political and economic reforms that both would further U.S. government policy and are consistent with the interests of the private sector. "The art of encouraging reforms by helping American business leaders advocate directly to foreign officials is best described as 'commercial diplomacy,'" Secretary Pritzker wrote. The secretary of commerce is best positioned to bring this perspective before the president and the NSC and to be the liaison to the business community on which such "commercial diplomacy" depends.

b. The secretary of homeland security is also often absent from the NSC table. This is also a mistake. The Department of Homeland Security (DHS) brings a transactional, decentralized, bottom-up, domestic perspective from a department that is integrally connected to communities, municipalities, state governments, and the private sector across the United States. This perspective can serve as a useful counterpoint to the more centralized, top-down, hierarchical approach that characterizes the traditional national security establishment. And DHS can complement the overseas ties of the national security and foreign policy departments and agencies with its own strong state and local, public and private sector relationships.

c. Participation of other department and agency heads at the NSC table needs to be addressed as well. The most glaring need identified by the ASG was to better integrate the nation's national security agenda with its international economic agenda—including trade, investment, sanctions, economic assistance, international financing, energy and commodities, monetary policy, and export controls. Bringing the secretaries of treasury and commerce, the U.S. trade representative, and other economic officials consistently to the NSC table will help.

There also needs to be closer coordination and often joint meetings between the NSC and the National Economic Council (NEC), especially at the principals and deputies levels. And the current practice of key NSC and NEC staff members dual-reporting to the heads of these two councils needs to continue. In the view of many people, the United States is using less effectively economic instruments for its geopolitical purposes than its global competitors, particularly China and Russia. While there are economic costs and risks to "economic statecraft" for both government policy and the commercial sector, there was a generally accepted view that this is an area of opportunity for U.S. policy. But making better use of geo-economic pressure for geopolitical gain will require dramatically increased coordination across the U.S. government and with U.S. friends and allies.

d. Also identified was the need to better integrate the Office of Management and Budget (OMB) into the NSC interagency policy development and executive process. This will help ensure that before the president adopts a policy initiative, he or she can be assured that it can be fully funded—that policy and resources will be fully aligned. The broader goal here is to ensure that the necessary officials are at the NSC table so that effective strategies can be developed and resourced using all sources of national power and influence.

e. Also too often missing from the NSC table is the secretary of energy. Yet with the continuing geopolitical importance of energy (especially oil, gas, and nuclear), our own continued dependence on energy imports (despite enhanced fracking and horizontal drilling), the role played by energy in global climate change, and the continued importance of nuclear deterrence and efforts to stem nuclear proliferation (and the Energy Department's central role in these matters), the energy secretary could make an essential contribution at many NSC meetings.

f. Adding the commerce, homeland security, and energy secretaries, along with other cabinet and agency officials, to the NSC table has the added advantage of bringing state and local governments, communities, and the private sector into the NSC system and process.

Similarly, civil society groups need to be brought more fully into the NSC process. If due respect and consideration is given to the fact that their interests do not always align with those of the federal government, these groups can in many cases provide crucial tools in developing not just "whole of government" but "whole of society" approaches to the challenges and opportunities the nation faces. But such an effort will require building (especially in the case of civil society) and rebuilding (in the case of social media and internet companies) a relationship of trust with the U.S. government.

9. Invest in the underdeveloped, nonmilitary instruments for national power and influence. Since the end of the Vietnam War, the United States has made a major investment of effort and resources in its military—its recruitment, training, equipping, exercising, effective deployment, and improvement through an intensive post-deployment "lessons learned" process. The result is the best military in the world by far.

But no similar effort has been made in developing the nonmilitary instruments of American power and influence—especially those largely civilian capabilities of peace-building, reconciliation, and conflict avoidance that seek to head off armed conflict—and the closely related largely civilian capabilities of post-conflict stabilization, reconciliation, and social and physical infrastructure reconstruction that are required to preserve the peace. These capabilities help train police in democratic and community-focused law enforcement; help train judges, prosecutors, and penal system administrators to respect and apply the rule of law; help governments and societies throw off corruption; help jump-start economic growth and job creation; and help enhance the ability of governments at every level to provide services (power, water, transportation, education, and health care) to their people.

It is fashionable now in both American political parties to foreswear "nation-building abroad." And America cannot "build" another nation—only the government and people of that nation can do so. But America and its friends and allies can help—and in some circumstances it is very much in their interest to do so. The Middle East is one of those circumstances.

ISIS will ultimately be cleared from the territory it now occupies in Syria and Iraq. But if the people of those two countries (and the people of other countries in the Middle East racked by violence and threatened by terrorists, such as Libya and Yemen) are unable to build stable, secure, and prosperous societies, they will inevitably become hosts to successor terrorist groups that will be even more virulent than ISIS—as ISIS was an even more virulent successor to al-Qaeda.

The United States simply does not have the civilian capabilities it needs to help nations and peoples threatened by or emerging from conflict or terrorism to build more secure, stable, and prosperous societies. Recently, each time the nation has been faced with such a requirement (as in Bosnia, Afghanistan, and Iraq) it has tried to make due with ad hoc, off-the-shelf capabilities and resources that have generally not been up to the task and have not produced the hoped-for success. The United States simply can no longer accept the national security consequences of this level of non-success—it simply must begin to resource the development, training, and equipping of these largely civilian capabilities.

In addition to these capabilities, Peter Feaver and Will Inboden, in an article circulated to the ASG, identified two other gaps in the U.S. foreign and defense policy toolkit that need to be addressed: first, the need to improve the Military Assistance Programs for training, equipping, and supporting the military and other security forces of countries that the United States wishes to help; second, "building an institutional ability to wage ideological warfare," especially in the "battle of ideas" against the propaganda of terrorist extremists like ISIS and al-Qaeda and of aggressive authoritarian regimes like Russia and China.

10. Build in informal, unstructured interactions. The formality of the NSC process—and of NSC meetings with the president in the Situation Room—can sometimes be a barrier to the kind of informal, candid discussion that an issue—and the president—actually need before the issue—and the president—are ready for decision.

The goal of the NSC process should be to get the president to the point where the president is satisfied that he or she has received all the relevant intelligence, expert analysis, and other information (from a variety of sources); has heard the views of all the relevant NSC principals; has received a full range of outside inputs (from experts, Congress, and the public); and is comfortable making a decision.

To meet this goal will usually require multiple meetings and conversations with the president in a variety of settings and formats—formal and informal—in the run-up to a decision. It is the responsibility of the NSC process—and particularly of the NSA—to make sure this goal is achieved to the president's satisfaction.

As an element of this process, in the second term of the George W. Bush administration, I instituted a regular Tuesday afternoon meeting in the NSA's office attended by the vice president; the White House chief of staff (invited but often unable to attend); the secretaries of state, defense, and treasury; the chairman of the joint chiefs of staff; the director of national intelligence; the director of central intelligence; and the deputy NSA. (Soft drinks, tortilla chips, and warmed cheese dip were served, which were found to improve the disposition of all the participants.)

In these meetings, the group would work through the most difficult and sensitive national security issues (like the Iran nuclear program, the Syrian nuclear reactor, North Korea's nuclear program). The limited representation (and limited dissemination of even the fact of these meetings) encouraged candid and in-depth discussions that were some of the best of the administration. And there were no leaks.

Once the issue had been worked through in this forum, the question (usually posed by Vice President Cheney) was how to take the issue to the president (something the NSA then worked out with the White House chief of staff). If the issue was ready for a formal decision, then an NSC meeting in the Situation Room; if a formal discussion short of a decision was best, then perhaps a meeting of NSC principals in the Oval Office; and if the goal was to have the president in more of a listening mode, then an informal meeting in the White House residence perhaps on a Saturday morning.

The point is that the process for bringing decisions to the president—and preparing the president to make those decisions—needs to be flexible and tailored to the issue, the need at the time, and the decision style of the president.

11. Bring in voices from the outside. There needs to be a formal, regular process for bringing in voices from outside the NSC system or it just will not happen. I did this selectively as NSA on Afghanistan and Iraq (especially in the run-up to President Bush's "Surge" decision in January 2007). But few NSAs did this as consistently and regularly as Tom Donilon during the Obama administration.

The current deputy NSA, Avril Haines, has been bringing in outsiders to meet with the Deputies Committee. This is a very good idea, worthy of imitation by the incoming administration. The NSA, NSC principals, and NSC deputies could all benefit from this kind of exposure. But even more important, the president should have structured, regular exposure to input, ideas, and views from people outside of the NSC (and outside of the intelligence community), reflecting a wide range of different backgrounds and perspectives.

12. Form, focus, train, and coach an expert NSC staff. A president needs to be clear on the mission the president intends for the NSC staff. The principal purposes of the NSC staff are to:

(1) support the president in carrying out the president's constitutional responsibilities in national and homeland security, and foreign, economic, and defense policy (e.g., help prepare the president for foreign leader meetings, foreign trips, speeches, foreign leader phone calls, and presidential decisions in these areas);

(2) champion presidential initiatives within the interagency (for if the president's NSC staff does not push the president's agenda, no one else will);

(3) coordinate and lead the interagency process in preparing for presidential decision issues that require input and action from multiple departments and agencies (e.g., developing analysis, clarifying options, gathering views); and

(4) coordinate and oversee the interagency implementation and execution of presidential decisions.

NSC senior directors need to understand that if they or their offices are doing things that do not fall into one of these categories, they should STOP—they are usurping the prerogatives and responsibilities of the line department and agencies. As already mentioned, the NSC staff needs to be self-disciplined and self-limiting regarding power—and not reaching to take control of things just because it can.

If this is the right set of functions for the NSC staff, then they probably can be accomplished with 100 to 150 professional staff with the right kind of experience—senior professionals drawn from the full range of national and homeland security and foreign, defense, and economic departments and agencies. But form should follow function—the size of the staff should be driven by its mission, and not by fiat or some arbitrary number. As a general proposition, it is better to have more information in fewer heads—to help the NSC staff members better identify trends, connections, and priorities.

In addition, an important purpose of the NSC staff is to integrate across the organizational stovepipes all too present in the departments and agencies of the interagency. This requires the NSC staff to function as a flat organization—sharing information, sharing credit, and working in task force mode—bringing together all the relevant NSC staff members on an issue. This is difficult to do if the NSC staff is too large and therefore tends to reproduce within itself the stovepipes of the interagency.

As the ASG papers on the "Third Offset" and "Moving to an Information Age Construct" made clear, it is the commercial sector where technical innovation essential to our future military and national security is happening. So the NSC needs to draw some of its staff from the relevant commercial sectors. Perhaps the best way to do this will be to find a way to rotate technical people from the commercial sector into the departments and agencies of our government—including the NSC staff—and similarly to rotate government personnel into the relevant commercial sectors.

Further, steps must also be taken to make it easier for commercial technology companies (including start-ups) to provide innovative technology to the government. There are a lot of differences that mitigate somewhat the applicability of lessons drawn from the private sector to government. But both need to put the highest priority on investing in their people—something the federal government (outside of the military) does not do well.

A number of practices from the private sector could improve the performance and morale of the NSC staff. Surprisingly, the NSC staff receives very little training. The assumption is that staff members come to the NSC fully trained by their parent departments and agencies. But the NSC staff is a specialized organization with a unique set of functions. Staff members coming to the NSC need to be trained for the specific tasks, responsibilities, and processes for which they will be responsible—and the manner and approach they should adopt in carrying them out. To test and further develop this training, periodic crisis response exercises should be conducted with the staff.

Many useful practices should be adopted that focus on improving the quality of senior managers and the leadership they provide to the workforce. These include:

(1) 360 degree reviews (so managers are aware of their evaluations not only by their superiors but also by their peers and subordinates).

(2) Professional coaches for senior managers that provide ongoing counsel and advice on how managers are perceived by others, how to compensate for their weaknesses, how to maximize their strengths, and how they can more effectively lead the organization.

The goal would be for the NSC staff to become a "learning organization" that advances the skills and performance of its people.

One final point made by several members of the ASG: the president and the NSA should ensure that persons detailed to the NSC are not disadvantaged in their career progression or otherwise penalized when they return to their home department or agency after service on the NSC staff. On the contrary, there is a lot of evidence that service on the NSC actually makes for more effective foreign service, intelligence, or military officers.

Conclusion

What is proposed here is a dramatic rolling back of how the NSC interagency system has come to operate over the last several administrations. Only the president can fix it.

A president gets the NSC system that the president deserves. It is the president's vehicle, and the president's responsibility. It is the view of most members of the ASG that the NSC system—and the interagency process—as they have evolved over the last couple decades are broken and are not meeting the needs of the president or the nation. If they are to be fixed, the new president must do the fixing.

The list of suggestions outlined above is a long one and may be simply too much for "the system" to digest at one time. If that is deemed to be the case, then the new president could adopt a more incremental approach. For example, the new president could pick four or five of the most urgent initiatives likely to have the biggest impact on the system—adopt them, evaluate their impact over time, adjust as necessary, and then adopt three or four more follow-on initiatives to continue the reform process. The four or five most urgent, potentially highest impact initiatives are probably numbers 3, 4, 6, 7, and 12 above.

As a separate matter, the whole issue of how to incorporate the "new domain" of cyber into U.S. strategy, planning, and operations both military and nonmilitary needs urgent and intensive further study. A White House task force is probably required to establish basic principles, a policy framework, departmental and agency responsibilities, and a coordination mechanism. The commission headed by Tom Donilon has an opportunity to play this role. Implementation and execution should then devolve to the relevant departments and agencies, under traditional NSC monitoring and oversight.

Finally, a blue-ribbon congressional/executive commission is very much in order to examine and make recommendations about how the two branches of government can work together more effectively to provide the nation a more agile, timely, and cutting-edge approach to a national strategy that integrates national and homeland security, and foreign, defense, and economic policy.

Stephen J. Hadley is a principal of RiceHadleyGates LLC, an international strategic consulting firm founded with Condoleezza Rice, Robert Gates, and Anja Manuel. Mr. Hadley is also Board Chairman of the United States Institute of Peace (USIP), and executive vice chair of the Board of the Atlantic Council. Mr. Hadley served for four years as the Assistant to the President for National Security Affairs from 2005 - 2009. From 2001 to 2005, Mr. Hadley was the Assistant to the President and Deputy National Security Advisor, serving under then National Security Advisor Condoleezza Rice. During his professional career, Mr. Hadley has served on a number of corporate and advisory boards, including: the National Security Advisory Panel to the Director of Central Intelligence, the Department of Defense Policy Board, and the State Department's Foreign Affairs Policy Board.

"Whatever the degree of difficulty, an upfront investment in effective organizational dynamics will pay dividends, particularly if addressed at an early stage."

—TOM PRITZKER

Investing in Effective Organizational Dynamics at the National Security Council

Tom Pritzker
Executive Chairman
Hyatt Hotels Corporation

A number of knowledgeable commentators at the ASG session referred to what seems to be an adage: "the president gets the NSC that he or she deserves." I have no view. From an outsider's perspective, "getting it right" in the case of National Security Council (NSC) staff and organization looks to be one of the more difficult endeavors I have run across. Whatever the degree of difficulty, an upfront investment in effective organizational dynamics will pay dividends, particularly if addressed at an early stage. This paper is an effort to articulate some thoughts and examples of tools that can potentially improve the organizational dynamics of the NSC.

My experience is limited to the private sector and therefore may embed ideas that are not appropriate for the NSC. On the other hand, the common element of all organizations is that people will drive results. Therefore, investing in people is investing in results.

Like any organization, the NSC has a set of characteristics that need to be considered when designing an approach to its human capital. Among those characteristics are the facts that the NSC is part of a political process and, at the NSC, time is an unusually scarce resource. Both of these characteristics have components of reality and elements of excuse. Being respectful of the former and skeptical of the latter are at the core of leadership. It is also incumbent on leadership to not allow the urgent to overwhelm the important. Over time, ignoring the important will have material consequences.

Dealing with human behaviors is neither fun nor within the experience base of some leadership teams. In the private sector (and the military), there is no alternative. It is forced on us, and because of its importance, it comes with the turf. While I understand that service in the NSC can be a pressure cooker, it would seem that where the stakes are highest is where effective behaviors and dynamics should be most valued. Finally (and I will find a way to say this three times), investing in human capital needs to be a priority from the top or it will not overcome the forces of inertia.

Let's start this assessment with some context. Here, I want to compare the motivations and alignment of individuals and teams within the private sector to those in the public sector. This is meant to highlight some of the challenges specific to the NSC and perhaps give some insights into crafting tools for the NSC.

1. **The individual.** In every organization, it is all about the people. To an even greater degree it is about the individuals in the leadership team whose behaviors and norms will establish the culture of the organization. Results are determined not just by the intelligence and knowledge of the individuals, but by their motivations, alignments, and behaviors. In order to make judgments about managing the NSC, we first need to understand the dynamics at the level of the individual. In terms of motivation, I would suspect that the population at the NSC is highly motivated. Their mission is important, and they can see a direct correlation between their work and the security of our country. For most, it doesn't get any better than that. Typically, the private sector cannot match these stakes nor this level of motivation, focus, and dedication.

   In terms of alignment of interests, the private sector probably has an advantage. In the private sector, individuals usually expects to have a long tenure with their company and their colleagues (although that is changing with millennials). They also expect their company to share responsibility for their career development. These characteristics can make individuals "owners" rather than "renters" of their jobs. It is my impression that tenure at the NSC is far shorter than job tenure in the private sector. In addition, when working in a senior government job, the individual is largely on his or her own in terms of nurturing personal career development. While people at the NSC are less likely to "own" their job, they are likely to be more singular in "owning" their careers. If this is accurate, it is also likely that the individual is surrounded by associates who also expect to have a relatively short tenure in their job and have a real awareness of the need to own their careers.

   A short-term mindset in any walk of life is just different. Knowing that you are going to have another career move in the near future will also have consequences. In addition, the daily regimen of an NSC job is often brutal in terms of stress on both the individuals and their families. It does not require much imagination to see that these dynamics will change the alignment, focus, and incentives of individuals within the NSC.

My purpose in making these observations is not to argue that these are good or bad, right or wrong. It is to provoke thought about how to manage individuals and teams in the context of the NSC. Here it might be worth noting that the military, although clearly a public service, shares certain dynamics with the private sector that we would be less likely to see within the NSC. The most obvious examples of this are expected job tenure and an intense organizational focus on human development.

2. **Team.** Creating an environment for effective teamwork requires constant attention. If left unattended, teamwork is likely to deteriorate over time. Starting from a conceptual perspective, there needs to be a common (and preferably well-articulated) understanding of purpose, strategy, and values. There should also be a philosophy in terms of span of control and distribution of authority. As these evolve, it is important to have multiple tools for clear communications. In terms of personal performance in a team setting, trust and well-articulated behavioral norms are the gold standards for effective teamwork.

During the ASG conference, there were several references to the importance of trust. Here, I would comment that alignment of interest, transparency, and duration of relationships are the feedstock for trust. The nature of the NSC, as discussed above, may create a shortage of these elements. To compensate, demanding adherence to certain behavioral norms can be important. At the first instance of deviation, a comment coupled with role modeling is appropriate. An example would be creating an environment where it is "safe" to thoughtfully say what is on your mind. Another example would be to have leadership demand that mutual respect be practiced. One can easily imagine how teamwork could be negatively affected by behavioral norms that go in the other direction. To some this may sound Pollyannaish, but teams are composed of individuals, and I cannot emphasize enough that an individual's emotions will impact not only his or her work product, but also the team's work product. Modern science (e.g., the field of behavioral economics) confirms that it is unrealistic to assume that humans (even really smart humans) will act rationally with no influence from their emotional makeup. The idea that emotions should be constantly repressed in favor of rationality is equally unrealistic. Importantly, this phenomenon does not necessarily disappear with seniority.

3. **Metrics and measurements.** Here, the private sector organization has the benefit of the common metric of financial performance. Most modern companies, however, go beyond this and create other metrics that may be referred to as management by objectives (MBOs). These allow supervisors to establish nonfinancial objectives that may relate to the development of human capital (theirs or that of their subordinates), the success of specific projects, etc. The world of the NSC may not lend itself to these sorts of tools. Clearly, linking performance to monetary incentives is not a tool available in government work.

The notes above are meant to provide context and a word of caution about simply importing private sector practices into the NSC. At the same time, the NSC is not immune from human dynamics. Understanding the natural state of those dynamics and then developing approaches to funnel those human dynamics into the desired results will take thought and effort. In the end, it is all about the people, their behaviors, and their abilities.

There are a number of different tools that can be crafted for the NSC. Each serves a different purpose and a different segment of the NSC population. Some can be outsourced, but each element should be designed as part of a total blueprint for managing the human dynamics of the NSC.

1. **Orientation**. Most organizations develop an orientation or onboarding program that can vary in length and content. The orientation program provides what may be a unique opportunity to establish a consistent message and common experience for the entire NSC staff. The purpose of the orientation program should be to set a common understanding of the administration's expectations of the NSC. It should create the context for the work of the NSC. Subject matter may include the NSC's purpose, structure, values, and operating guidelines, but should also include information about the specific ideas, philosophies, and strategies of the leadership in the White House. It should be mandatory for all employees upon entering the NSC. It should be viewed as the beginning of an onboarding process. There may also be training blocks attached to the basic orientation package that are offered only to (or required of) specific cohorts within the NSC.

2. **Training**. Training programs are about building specific skills, such as writing, research, protocols, processes, etc. It can also be more contextual and involve understanding the larger picture of policy making. In all cases, training is meant to close gaps that need to be closed. Identifying gaps is critical to this process. These are tools to support identifying these gaps. I suspect that those who have been involved with the NSC will be better positioned to articulate common gaps as well as opportunities for improvement.

3. **Testing**. Personality assessment (e.g., Caliper test) is mandated for all executives above a certain level at Hyatt and in many other companies in the private sector. This is an online questionnaire, which generates information regarding an individual's communication skills and style, emotional intelligence, mental agility and resilience, and cultural fit. The results effectively unbundle and precisely articulate these aspects of an individual's personality. Few people will be surprised by the results. However, the unbundled nature of the results increases the individual's awareness of the details and enables behavioral modifications where appropriate. It also gives people the opportunity to find workarounds or structures to support their individual performance.

4. **Coaching**. Unlike training, coaching tends to be oriented toward affective behaviors. It addresses how behaviors can improve or impair impact. Impact is not just designing good policy, it also involves implementation and that depends on people. Coaching basically raises your awareness and insights into your own style. It is meant to enable you to change your behaviors in order to achieve different and hopefully better results. Coaching comes in different forms depending on the need. There are coaches for communications, performance, and professional transitions, as well as executive coaching. Each is different. Below, I address executive coaching, which is typically used by the more senior executives who have already been successful. It is meant to improve the styles, abilities, and impact of individuals who are clearly qualified for their job.

My own experience with coaching began ten years ago. I had an issue with a senior executive and decided to look into coaching. Before asking this senior executive to work with a coach, I researched the experience by asking my closest senior business colleague to join me in being coached. We each took a short series of tests that profiled our personality preferences and our styles of leadership. I need to emphasize here that these tests are not about right and wrong nor smart and dumb, they uncover individual traits, styles, and challenges. What each of us learned about ourselves wasn't new, but it was both unbundled and more precisely articulated than our minds typically allow. This enabled each of us to better understand the separate elements of our behaviors.

I can report two distinct outcomes from this research effort. First, it has materially improved how the two of us work together as a team. Second, and perhaps most importantly, each of us has found that we are trainable in terms of moderating our behaviors.

The epilogue to this story is that the senior executive in question was unable to adapt to the needed changes in our organization, and this quickly became apparent from his profiles and a short engagement with a coach. He recognized that he was a square peg in a round hole. Soon thereafter he came to me and suggested that he was not the right person for the job. This process avoided a potentially costly train wreck.

While executive coaching is increasingly being used at senior levels in companies, it is not yet commonly understood, so I will give some examples of insights one might gain from the profiles. On its most conceptual level, the tests give you a personality assessment and a preference inventory. They describe your instinctive responses to situations. From this, coaching can provide you with insights into how others hear you and experience you, how you typically behave "in the moment," and how you might be more effective in your style of management and communication. Below are a few examples of profiles that might come out of the assessment tools.

a. High assertiveness, high aggressiveness, and high ego drive. This might suggest someone who is not very good at listening and who may be perceived as inaccessible by subordinates or arrogant by team members. These attributes are not fatal, but self-awareness of these traits can allow this person manage how he or she is being perceived.

b. High idea orientation, high abstract reasoning, high self-structure, and low flexibility. This might suggest someone who is not very agile in assimilating new information or diverse ideas. Understanding this about him or herself will allow this person to modify his or her instinctive response to a new idea or to a change of facts on the ground.

c. High idea orientation, high self-structure, high ego strength, low empathy. This is a very smart, creative, infectiously positive person who insists his or her people think outside of the box.

d. Low empathy, low assertiveness, low ego drive, low sociability, high abstract reasoning. This is a very smart person who prefers to intellectualize or analyze but isn't a people person. This person will likely not be an effective leader but rather rely on data trends when making a decision.

As a simple example of executive coaching, one could imagine a coach observing that his or her client should avoid using "hot" or "demeaning" words in a discussion. This would be an example of a reasonably easy opportunity to mitigate a behavior in order to have more impact on outcomes.

Here are three value adds from executive coaching.

a. It can help provide an objective view of yourself and how you impact others. People in senior positions are unlikely to get this feedback without a coach.

b. It can provide feedback on how you behave in the moment. If someone is perceived as too aggressive or dismissive, it can damage both individual and team dynamics. For a senior person, it is very hard to undo that damage. A coach can help you set the tone and the norms of behavior that you will role model and that you should expect (and demand) from your teams.

c. Getting quite granular, a coach can also help with phrases, words, and role-playing to help you have the desired impact and be received consistent with your intent. How you present will inform how you expect others to present. This will set the environment for both decision-making and policy implementation.

If orientation programs are for all members of the NSC and training is for a subset, then executive coaching is most effective with senior leadership. The conundrum, of course, is that members of senior leadership have the highest demand on their time. The paradox is that the more senior you get, the more benefit a coach can bring. Because the more seniority you have, the more impact your voice, tone, and choice of words will have—for good or for bad.

In terms of the judgments we have made at Hyatt, we mandate coaching for the executive chairman, the CEO and the CEO's direct reports. Coaching is a continuous process that does not have a beginning and an end, although it is front-end loaded in terms of time commitment. I am told that at Goldman Sachs, the mandate starts with the CEO and reaches deep into the organization. Coaching has become increasingly common in well-run companies. Amongst my peers, it is well accepted that the role modeling of having a coach must start at the top. Further, we mandate certain testing for new hires above a certain level. We believe that understanding an individual's foibles can help avoid the much feared train wreck that can be time-consuming and take on a dynamic all its own. Having worked in a number of organizations, from start-ups to mature companies, I have no doubt that NSC staff will respond to behavioral models and tone at the top. This is why executive coaching is most effective at the top.

5. **Feedback.** Some form of structured feedback is important. It is a moment for both the supervisor and the subordinate to reflect on successes and on opportunities for improvement. Whatever feedback loop is used, it should be executed in a fashion that is understandable and is structured to stand apart from the heat of the daily routine.

The functional expectations of the NSC could not be more important, nor more demanding for the individuals involved. There are a number of opportunities for investing in the effectiveness of the NSC. Traditionally these might include technology, streamlining processes, communication systems, etc. In the end, however, people will drive results, and the opportunity to invest in people should not be overlooked. A comprehensive approach to human capital can have a huge return on investment. Where an organization knows that it will be under constant stress, having a well-defined approach in place early can provide tools for identifying risks and opportunities as well as tools for improved organizational effectiveness.

Investments in orientation, training, testing, coaching, or feedback will impact the human capital that is at the heart of the NSC. Each of the tools discussed serves a different function, and those functions should not be conflated. Once an approach to human resources is constructed, the process of continuous improvement can begin. I did not provide here an exhaustive list of tools (e.g., I have not discussed 360 reviews and other potential tools). Rather, my purpose was to stimulate discussion around the idea that there are modern tools that can be employed to enhance the performance and operations of the NSC in the next administration. These will not cure all ills, but they will begin to allow the leadership team to more surgically identify opportunities and threats to the effective operation of the NSC.

Tom Pritzker is Executive Chairman of Hyatt Hotels Corporation, Chairman of the Center for Strategic and International Studies in Washington, DC, and a member of the Aspen Strategy Group.

"One of the traditional functions of the diplomat has been the representation of the U.S. abroad: explaining and advocating U.S. policy, reporting on external developments, and negotiating on behalf of the U.S. This role, too, has eroded over time."

—JAMES B. STEINBERG

Present at the "Re-Creation": The Role of the State Department in Formulating and Implementing U.S. Global Policy

James B. Steinberg
Professor
Syracuse University

In recent years it has become increasingly commonplace to lament the declining role of the State Department in the formulation and implementation of U.S. national security policy.[1] This trend has been attributed to a number of factors, most notably: the growing size and scope of responsibility of the National Security Council (NSC) staff; declining budgets for State Department operations; emergence of nontraditional issues on the foreign policy agenda (terrorism, crime and drugs, climate change); enhanced roles for the military and CIA beyond traditional functions (civil affairs, diplomacy, development assistance); the expanded overseas presence of federal agencies other than State Department (Treasury, Homeland Security, FBI, Commerce); improved communications, which allows foreign policy to be conducted directly from capital to capital; and personnel (hiring and promotion) policies at State, among others. Many see the root of this trend in the adoption of the National Security Act of 1947, accelerating with the emergence of the assistant to the president for national security affairs (national security advisor) as a powerful policy maker, beginning in the Kennedy administration.[2] In the field, the Goldwater Nichols Act of 1986, which elevated the operational role of regional military commanders (COCOMS) has also had the effect of displacing State Department leadership in areas ranging from the Middle East (Central Command) to East Asia (PACOM) to Africa (AFRICOM).

It's hard to identify the claimed halcyon period of State Department primacy.[3] From the earliest days of American history, the president has played the key role in most major foreign policy decisions, and rarely has the White House delegated to the secretary of state and the State Department the principal responsibility for U.S. national security policy. Until World War II, when the State Department emerged in its modern form, the department remained very small, and many of its responsibilities had little or nothing to do with foreign affairs (for example, keeping the Great Seal of the United States). Although the United States has been fortunate to have had an impressive number of talented public servants/diplomats serve as secretary of state (Thomas Jefferson, John Quincy Adams, Daniel Webster, William Seward, John Hay, Charles Evans Hughes, Cordell Hull, George Marshall, Dean Acheson, Henry Kissinger, George Shultz, and Madeleine Albright to name but a few), on the paramount foreign policy issues of the day, they have largely played a supportive role. Key initiatives have often emanated from the White House, sometimes designed and executed by non-State Department personnel—think House, Hopkins, and Harriman as archetypes in the twentieth century. Indeed, relatively few secretaries of state have been the president's principal foreign policy advisor and confidant—though there have been notable exceptions, as in the case of President George H.W. Bush and Secretary James Baker.[4]

Thus sweeping proposals to establish the secretary of state as the "vicar" of U.S. foreign policy and to establish State Department primacy fly in the face of long historical experience. Yet there are important reasons to believe that the State Department can and should play a larger and more influential role in both policy development and execution. Its organizational capacity is far greater than what could ever be replicated at the NSC; its global presence is especially valuable in a world in which international relations involve not just governments and international organizations, but business, civil society, and wider publics, where firsthand engagement on the ground is invaluable and the range of its expertise can help facilitate integration of policy across regions and functional issues far better than agencies, which have a primary mission limited to one domain (trade, finance, agriculture, health, environment, terrorism, etc.). This ability to integrate across multiple objectives and policy instrument choices is the essence of "smart power."

A number of studies over the past two decades have suggested steps that could be taken to strengthen the role of the State Department, from the department's own efforts—in the Quadrennial Diplomacy and Development Reviews (QDDRs)—to outside groups.[5]

The department's unique character among the executive agencies presents both a challenge and an opportunity in seeking to define its appropriate role. Most of the other agencies are relatively specialized, and thus have a comparative substantive advantage on "their" issues—from finance (Treasury), business (Commerce), agriculture, trade, energy, health, military and intelligence, law enforcement, etc.

Moreover, these agencies have strong ties to influential domestic constituencies, and in many cases have strong backing from key committees in Congress. In the past, it might be argued that the State Department's specialization was "knowledge of foreign things," but with globalization, each of the specialized agencies has become quite sophisticated about the world within its own substantive realm, thus undercutting State's comparative advantage. In fact, the State Department's focus on the world outside the United States is seen by some as part of the rationale for State's diminished role—on the grounds that State is perceived by some as more focused on the needs and interests of foreign interlocutors than on zealously promoting U.S. national interests.[6]

So what does State bring to the table? To borrow Isaiah Berlin's metaphor, what arguably distinguishes State is that while the other agencies are hedgehogs, State is a fox.[7] Thus in seeking to define State's role, one starting place is to consider the comparative advantage of the fox in the design and execution of national security.

To evaluate the options for how this might be accomplished, it is useful to look across two key parameters of U.S. foreign policy—1) policy formulation versus policy implementation and 2) activities in Washington versus activities in the field. In developing proposals, we need to examine both the ways in which State's role in the interagency process might be reformed, and how the department itself should be reformed to play an enhanced role. These reforms could focus on the principal functions that the State Department has or could play:

1) State Department as convener

2) State Department as integrator

3) State Department as representative/negotiator[8]

State Department as Convener

One of the principal reasons for the growth of the NSC staff over the past two decades has been the prominence of the NSC in organizing the deliberations of the U.S. government. At every level of the process—interagency working groups/policy committees (IWG/IPC), involving deputies and principals, agendas are developed, meetings chaired, and taskers issued by NSC personnel. This development has been propelled by the idea that the NSC is the (and the only) "honest broker" in a system of bureaucratic actors, while all the others are special pleaders who seek to advance their distinctive institutional interest.[9] There is of course important validity to the bureaucratic interest model, but State's unique role arguably makes it reasonably well suited to act as an honest broker as well, with important built-in institutional capacity to do the preparatory and follow-up work to bring all the issues and options to the table and to assure that appropriate action is taken so that decisions are implemented.[10]

To take advantage of State's convening capacity, there should be a strong presumption in favor of the State Department chairing IWGs, particularly those with a heavy focus on policy implementation outside of Washington, with the NSC staff participating as vice chair, but largely playing the role of keeping key White House personnel informed of the deliberations and making sure that White House perspectives are reflected in the interagency deliberation. In recent years, we have occasionally seen the State Department play this role—the most frequently cited successful example is Plan Colombia, where the Undersecretary of State for Political Affairs Tom Pickering chaired the interagency group. There may be circumstances where another agency is better equipped to staff an IWG (e.g., Energy or Commerce), but generally the NSC should not play the lead. In addition to formal IWGs, state assistant secretaries should regularly and informally convene their interagency counterparts, modelled on Richard Holbrooke's "informals"[11] and the "deputies lunch."

This approach was the organizing principal behind National Security Action Memorandum 341 (March 2, 1966), "The Direction, Coordination and Supervision of Departmental Activities Overseas," issued under President Johnson, which gave the secretary of state "responsibility to the full extent permitted by law for the overall direction, coordination and supervision of interdepartmental activities overseas— primarily through the Under Secretary of State and the regional Assistant Secretaries of State, who will be assisted by the intergovernmental groups of which they will be executive chairman."[12] But the system was never fully implemented, and in practice, President Johnson relied primarily on informal mechanisms.[13]

Although the model could be applied in both policy formulation and policy implementation, it is especially compelling in the latter case, where the need to attend to day-to-day operational demands puts an extraordinary strain on a small staff like that of the NSC.

A variant of this approach would be to "dual-hat" the relevant State Department official with an NSC as well as State Department title. This approach could enhance the perceived authority and legitimacy of the chair within the interagency by conferring a White House imprimatur.[14]

The State Department's capacity to act as a convener is most clearly on display in U.S. missions abroad, where the ambassador and deputy chief of mission act as focal points for bringing together all of the resident agencies to implement policies decided in Washington. The fact that the chief of mission is dual-hatted as both the president's and the secretary of state's representative has helped facilitate the idea that the ambassador is the appropriate convener of all the relevant interests in the mission. A number of commentators have noted the erosion of the chief of mission authority in recent years and have called for a reaffirmation, and even strengthening, of the role.[15]

State as Integrator

Closely related, but a somewhat more radical change would be to elevate the role of the State Department as policy integrator—having State play the primary role in the development of policy options papers and implementation plans for the national security apparatus. There are precedents for this—for example, in the early years after the establishment of the Office of Policy Planning at State, the papers prepared by the staff were for the direct consumption of the president.[16] During the Balkan conflict, Assistant Secretary Holbrooke not only regularly convened all the relevant agencies on a regular basis, but also prepared the policy papers for higher-level interagency consideration. In recent years this policy integration function has migrated heavily to the White House—as, for example, in the role of the deputy national security advisor for Iraq and Afghanistan. Similarly, a number of studies have called for strengthening the strategic planning capacity of the NSC. While the need for more effective strategic planning is apparent, in principal this effort could be led by State, with participation by all relevant agencies.[17]

State as Representative

One of the traditional functions of the diplomat has been the representation of the U.S. abroad: explaining and advocating U.S. policy, reporting on external developments, and negotiating on behalf of the U.S. This role, too, has eroded over time. The spread of rapid, reliable, and secure communications between capitals has allowed governments to cut out the "middle man" of the foreign mission. The emergence of NSC-like structures in key foreign governments means that more and more business is transacted with White House rather than State Department/Foreign

Ministry counterparts (e.g., 10 Downing Street, Germany's "Kanzerleramt," Japan's Kantei). The expansion of non-State personnel abroad (either stationed at the embassy or commuting from DC) has led to more direct engagement by other executive agencies, bypassing State. On many important international negotiations (especially, but not limited to, economic issues), delegations are led either by White House or other executive agency personnel. Appointment of ambassadors with limited foreign policy experience, substantive knowledge, and stature has also undercut the chief of mission's ability to function as the primary U.S. representative in country.

A second dimension of the "representation" role is in the context of international negotiations. In the past, the State Department and State personnel have often led U.S. negotiating delegations across a wide variety of substantive issues. For example, from 1981-1992, the U.S. "Sherpa" to the G7 summit (representing the president) was the undersecretary of state for economic affairs.[18] The U.S. special envoy for climate change, who represents the U.S. at international climate negotiations, is a State Department official. Civil aviation agreements are negotiated by State; State co-leads negotiations for bilateral investment treaties with the United States trade representative, and with the merger of the Arms Control and Disarmament Agency into State, much of the arms control negotiations have been led from State. State negotiates status of forces agreements for the U.S. military. Sustaining State's leadership role in negotiations is an appropriate and necessary complement to strengthening its convening and integrating role in policy, while the NSC and specialized agencies can focus on negotiation back-up, staff support, and technical expertise—a model that was followed during the Iran nuclear negotiations. Having State lead negotiating delegations is a natural complement to the convening function and plays to the strength of State personnel, who can place the negotiations on particular issues within the broader context of overall U.S. national security goals.

One crucial aspect of the representation function is "representation" to broader elements of societies abroad—business, civil society, media, etc.—broadly grouped under public diplomacy. There has been considerable effort both to increase State's capacity to engage in twenty-first century public diplomacy and "strategic communications," but here too the tendency has been for capacity and focus to migrate to the White House and other agencies, especially Defense. It has become increasingly apparent that the U.S. needs stronger and more integrated strategic communications—and the State Department is the logical home for this effort.

Internal Organization

If the State Department is to play an enhanced role in policy formulation and implementation, with a particular emphasis on policy integration and representation of the United States overseas and in international fora, then the internal organization and focus of the department needs to reflect these roles.

Policy Integration: To facilitate the role of integrator, greater effort needs to be made to break down the stovepipes within the State Department, particularly across geographic bureaus and between regional and functional bureaus. There is a certain healthy tension between the regional bureaus, which reflects the political reality that most policy making abroad emerges from states and in some cases regional organizations, and the functional bureaus, which reflect the increasingly transnational character of many contemporary issues and require deep substantive expertise.

The most promising opportunities for integration exist at the "seventh floor" level. First, the role of the under secretaries should be strengthened to serve as a sort of policy coordination committee, rather than another layer of bureaucracy between the working bureaus and the secretary. Instead of focusing on day-to-day operations, the undersecretaries, who represent the broad range of substantive perspectives, should serve as a kind of internal deputies committee (perhaps even chaired by the policy deputy) not only to tee up decisions for the secretary, but also to strengthen the intellectual heft of the department's role in the interagency process. This committee could be staffed by Policy Planning and the Bureau of Intelligence and Research. Policy Planning staff's (S/P) own role as an integrator could be enhanced by formally requiring each bureau (regional and functional) to assign one individual to represent the perspective of the bureau in S/P's work, alongside experts from outside the State Department. S/P should also play a lead role in implementing two of the valuable proposals of the 2016 QDDR, the increased use of data, and lessons learned in policy development and implementation. The proposed hub is moving in the right direction, but without some formal institutional linkage to the department's day-to-day work, these proposals may have a limited impact.

Policy Implementation: The need for integration is equally compelling on the operational/implementation level, especially in the field and for complex contingencies that include military assets.[19] For a number of reasons, this integration/coordination function has tended to migrate to the COCOMs, in part for resource reasons. The creation of the Bureau of Conflict and Stabilization Operations was designed to help strengthen the State Department's ability to play a leadership role in these operations, but a lack of resources and willingness to back this effort wholeheartedly has led to serious underperformance.

Representation: There needs to be a strengthened focus on the selection and training of senior mission personnel and a willingness of the secretary of state to invest his or her personal authority in acting through them. The 2010 QDDR emphasized the importance of this role. This should be coupled with a more active role for regional and functional assistant secretaries in the field—as key interlocutors with both government and nongovernmental actors, while leaving the day-to-day bureau administration primarily to the principal deputy assistant secretaries.

Public Diplomacy: As noted above, public diplomacy is an especially critical feature of representation. State's lead role in executing public diplomacy should be reaffirmed and strengthened. Public diplomacy considerations need to have a seat at the table from the outset of policy design, rather than being an afterthought after policy is already adopted.

Resources and People

This paper has focused on structural and process actions that can help State play a more effective role in the design and executions of U.S. national security strategy. But none of this can be achieved without adequate resources and skilled, trained, and motivated people. It is an all too common refrain that diplomacy is under-resourced compared with other tools in the national security kitbag, but the need for a comprehensive budgeting policy that integrates all the national security functions (050 and 150) both within the executive branch and in the congressional appropriation process remains a critical unmet need.

Ultimately the strength of State is its people—a highly dedicated, motivated, and talented group of foreign service officers, civil servants, and locally engaged staff. Although the career model remains critical to the long-term development of personnel, more flexibility in hiring and the promotion of shorter-term individuals at mid-career with needed skills from business, civil society, and the academy would help State adapt more effectively to a fast-changing international environment. For career personnel, greater training opportunities, modeled on the comprehensive approach taken by the military, would also promote a more effective, adaptable workforce.

James B. Steinberg is University Professor of Social Science, International Affairs and Law at Syracuse University and served as Dean of the Maxwell School from July 2011 until June 2016. Prior to becoming Dean on July 1, 2011, he served as Deputy Secretary of State, serving as the principal Deputy to Secretary Clinton. From 2005 to 2008 Mr. Steinberg was Dean of the Lyndon B. Johnson School of Public Affairs. From 2001 to 2005, he was vice president and director of Foreign Policy Studies at the Brookings Institution, where he supervised a wide-ranging research program on U.S. foreign policy. Mr. Steinberg served as deputy national security advisor to President Clinton from 1996 to 2000. During that period he also served as the president's personal representative to the 1998 and 1999 G-8 summits. Prior to becoming deputy national security advisor, Mr. Steinberg served as director of the State Department's policy planning staff, and as deputy assistant secretary for analysis in the Bureau of Intelligence and Research. Mr. Steinberg's most recent book is *Strategic Reassurance and Resolve: US-China Relations in the 21st Century with Michael O'Hanlon* (Princeton University Press, winter 2014). He has also authored *Difficult Transitions: Foreign Policy Troubles at the Outset of Presidential Power* (2008) with Kurt Campbell. Mr. Steinberg received his B.A. from Harvard and a J.D. from Yale Law School. He is a member of the Aspen Strategy Group.

[1] See for example, Goldfien, Michael. March 30, 2016. "How the NSC Hijacked U.S. Foreign Policy." *The National Interest*. http://nationalinterest.org/feature/how-the-nsc-hijacked-us-foreign-policy-15625

[2] Daalder, Ivo H., and I.M. Destler. 2009. *In the Shadow of the Oval Office: Profiles of the National Security Advisor and the Presidents They Served*. New York: Simon and Shuster.

[3] According to the State Department website (http://www.state.gov/r/pa/ei/rls/dos/436.htm), "As the lead foreign affairs agency, the Department of State has the primary role in

- Leading interagency coordination in developing and implementing U.S.foreign policy;
- Managing the foreign affairs budget and other foreign affairs resources;
- Leading and coordinating U.S. representation abroad. . . .
- Conducting negotiations and concluding agreements and treaties on issues ranging from trade to nuclear weapons;
- Coordinating and supporting international activities of other U.S. agencies and officials."

[4] The United States is not the only country where the titular lead agency for foreign policy has played a secondary role—as, for example, in the marginalization of the British foreign secretary under Prime Minister Lloyd George in the UK or the overshadowing of the Foreign Office by the German military under William II. See Craig, Gordon, and Felix Gilbert, eds. 1953. *The Diplomats 1919-1939*. Princeton, NJ: Princeton University Press, Chapter 1, "The British Foreign Office" (Gordon Craig) and Chapter 5, "Diplomats and Diplomacy in the Early Weimar Republic" (Hajo Holborn).

[5] U.S. Department of State. 2015. *Enduring Leadership in a Dynamic World, 2015 Quadrennial Diplomacy and Development Review*. http://www.state.gov/documents/organization/241429.pdf; U.S. Department of State. 2010. *Leading Through Civilian Power, The First Quadrennial Diplomacy and Development Review*. http://www.state.gov/documents/organization/153108.pdf; Council on Foreign Relations. 2001. *State Department Reform*. ("lodge under Presidential and National Security Council guidance, responsibility for foreign policy implementation within the Department of State; designate . . . the Secretary of State as principal spokesman on foreign policy for the president and his administration.") http://www.cfr.org/organization-of-government/state-department-reform/p9114; Chow, Eugene, and Richard Weitz. 2010. *Rebuilding Diplomacy*. Washington, DC: Center for a New American Security. http://www.cnas.org/

files/documents/publications/Rebuilding%20Diplomacy_Chow%20Weitz.pdf; Advisory Committee on Transformational Diplomacy. 2008. *Final Report of the State Department in 2025 Working Group.* http://2001-2009.state.gov/documents/organization/99879.pdf

[6] This caricature is well-expressed in the oft-repeated anecdote about Secretary of State George Shultz, who made it his practice to call newly appointed U.S. ambassadors into his office and ask them to point out their country on the large globe in his office. According to Shultz, they invariably pointed to the country to which they were to be posted, and Shultz, on reminding them that "their country" was the United States, replied: "Never forget what country you're representing." Nordlinger, Jay. February 11, 2008. "Around the World with George Shultz." *National Review.* http://www.nationalreview.com/article/343476/around-world-shultz-jay-nordlinger. Recent secretaries of state have sought to counter this image by promoting initiatives like the Office of Commercial and Business Affairs, which "coordinates State Department advocacy on behalf of American business."

[7] Berlin, Isaiah. 2013. *The Hedgehog and the Fox: An Essay on Tolstoy's View of History.* Princeton, NJ: Princeton University Press. It's perhaps notable that in a recent study, psychologist Philip Tetlock concluded that foxes were better at forecasting than hedgehogs. See Tetlock, P.E. 2005. *Expert Political Judgment: How Good Is It? How Can We Know?* Princeton, NJ: Princeton University Press.

[8] A possible fourth role is "State as enabler," focusing on how State can support and make more effective the work of other agencies by sharing expertise, perspective, and capacity. I am grateful to Professor Jeremy Weinstock for this suggestion during our ASG discussions.

[9] Halperin, Morton. 1974. *Bureaucratic Politics and Foreign Policy.* Washington, DC: Brookings Institution Press; Allison, Graham, and Philip Zelikow. 1999. Essence of Decision. New York: Longman.

[10] It might be argued that State is a special pleader for "diplomacy" as a preferred tool of policy, in contrast to other agencies that have their own preferred toolkit. But history suggests State has been as willing to advocate for the use of military and economic tools as the agencies who actually wield them—as well captured in the now famous exchange between then U.S. Permanent Representative to the UN Madeleine Albright and Chairman of the Joint Chiefs of Staff General Colin Powell over the use of force in the Balkans. See Powell, Colin. 1995. *My American Journey.* New York: Random House, 576.

[11] As assistant secretary of state for East Asia, Holbrooke brought together key Asia policy makers from NSC, Department of Defense, and CIA for weekly meetings in his office—see Rothkopf, David. 2005. *Running the World: The Inside Story of the National Security Council and the Architects of American Power.* New York: Public Affairs, 189—a practice he replicated as assistant secretary for Europe under President Clinton.

[12] The Undersecretaries Committee and IRG, chaired by State, were continued at the outset of the Nixon administration. See National Security Decision Memorandum 2. January 20, 1969. FRUS 1969-1976, Vol. 2, p. 30.

[13] See Herring, George C. 1994. *LBJ and Vietnam.* Austin, TX: University of Texas Press, 12-16.

[14] This approach was suggested by Dr. Joseph Nye, who in the Carter administration served as deputy to the undersecretary of state for security assistance but also chaired the NSC group on the non-proliferation of weapons.

[15] Advisory Committee on Transformational Diplomacy. 2008. *Final Report of the State Department in 2025 Working Group,* 21. http://2001-2009.state.gov/documents/organization/99879.pdf

[16] For example, NSC 68 (1950), "United States Objectives and Programs for National Security," was drafted by the State Department's Policy Planning Staff. See U.S. Department of State. 1977. *Foreign Relations of the United States, 1950, vol. 1.* Washington, DC: Government Printing Office, 234-292; Over time, "the locus of foreign policy planning shifted to the NSC." Bloomfield, Lincoln. 1978. "Planning Foreign Policy: Can it be Done?" *Political Science Quarterly* 93 (3): 373-374.

[17] There are precedents for this approach. For example, the report of the Commission on the Organization of the Government for the Conduct of Foreign Policy (the "Murphy Commission") from 1975 proposed that "the State Department should have the central role in the critical process of policy development and provide the necessary central coordination and leadership in the foreign affairs community." See Congressional Research Service. 1975. *Commission on the Organization of the Government for the Conduct of Foreign Policy: Background and Principal Recommendations*, 8. http://research.policyarchive.org/20213. pdf. The Working Group on Transformational Diplomacy made similar recommendations, with a particular focus on regional planning. See Advisory Committee on Transformational Diplomacy. 2008. *Final Report of the State Department in 2025 Working Group*, 18-20. http://2001-2009.state.gov/documents/organization/99879.pdf

[18] Mourlon-Druol, Emmanuel, and Federico Romero, eds. 2014. *International Summitry and Global Governance.* New York: Routledge, 73.

[19] The Bureau of Conflict and Stabilization Operations evolved out of the under-institutionalized Office of the Coordinator for Reconstruction and Stabilization—the objective was laid out first by the Advisory Committee on Transformational Diplomacy, which recommended that the State Department "[b]uild and institutionalize an integrated operational capability to respond rapidly to contingencies, support country transitions and create tangible results on the ground." Advisory Committee on Transformational Diplomacy. 2008. *Final Report of the State Department in 2025 Working Group*, 4. http://2001-2009.state. gov/documents/organization/99879.pdf. This idea was taken up in the 2010 QDDR.

[20] "We will work with other agencies to ensure that chiefs of missions can contribute to the evaluation of all personnel at post, engage directly in high-level policymaking in Washington DC, where possible and have clear reporting structures for all U.S. civilians in country."

[21] See Advisory Committee on Transformational Diplomacy. 2008. *Final Report of the State Department in 2025 Working Group*, 5-6. http://2001-2009.state.gov/documents/organization/99879.pdf

"In the end, the whole point of homeland security is to help create a safe, secure, and resilient place where the American way of life can thrive. Homeland security reveals the simple truth that the success of this task will depend as much on each of us as it will on us all."

—JANE HOLL LUTE

Rethinking the Architecture of U.S. National Security: Lessons from the Homeland[1]

Jane Holl Lute
Under Secretary General
United Nations

Introduction

Framing U.S. security needs in terms of the American "homeland" did not seem to preoccupy the great architects of the post-World War II order when they formalized, in the National Security Act of 1947, much of what we know today as the national security establishment of the federal government. Yet, the sweeping term—and the sprawling enterprise—that we now call "homeland security" has, nevertheless, come to occupy an essential place in the effort to ensure the foundational protection of American society.

Over the past nearly 15 years, everyone has heard of homeland security and the U.S. federal department that bears its name. Employing over one-quarter million federal civilian and military personnel, supported directly by nearly a quarter million more from the private sector, and ticking through a budget of well over $1 billion per week, the U.S. Department of Homeland Security (DHS) reaches far more widely and deeply than its federal workforce or dollars suggest. Over the last decade, over 1 million people have passed through DHS customs and border protection points each day, and an average of 2 million people every day have undergone aviation security screening—numbers overall that rival the population of the entire world. In that same time frame, hundreds of billions of dollars have been spent at the federal, state, and local levels, including, for example, over $100 billion in domestic disaster assistance for hurricanes alone.

---

1 This paper is presented by the author in her personal capacity. The opinions expressed in this article are the author's own and do not reflect the view of either the United Nations or the United States. This paper draws, in part, on ideas presented in previous work by the author who would like to thank Brian DeVallance, Thomas Winkowski, Rich Serino, John Cohen, and Dan Gerstein for their valuable input. Any errors remain the sole responsibility of the author.

These numbers are impressive, but just what have we learned from the creation, evolution, and operations of DHS? What does this relatively new frontier of national security have to teach us about how best to cope in our highly disrupted world? How can its concepts and architecture be leveraged to the fullest effect in the overall service of America's national interests and in the security of the American people?

Background

In 2002, almost fourteen years ago, Congress created DHS in a move that represented the most sweeping reorganization of the executive branch since just after World War II. Pieced together from the whole or parts of 22 departments, agencies, and offices under a thin veneer of administrative architecture, DHS was charged with shaping and focusing this disparate collection of vaguely associated responsibilities on the clearest of aims: to prevent another September 11th.

But clear aims do not always translate into clear lanes, and DHS lore recounts senior White House staff and colleagues going through pools of ink and piles of napkins as they drew and redrew the lines and boxes that would make up the third-largest department in the U.S. federal government. Important missions were divided into pieces, often on the thinnest of reasoning having little to do with substance: for example, responsibility for immigration and border crossings—but not visas—would go to DHS. The federal domestic law enforcement agencies of the Border Patrol, Customs, and Secret Service would move—but not the FBI; Bureau of Alcohol, Tobacco, Firearms and Explosives; or the Drug Enforcement Administration. The responsibility to secure the integrity of the nation's money supply would migrate to DHS, but not investigative oversight of major financial fraud.

From the outset, DHS faced significant strategic and operational hurdles. What did "homeland security" mean anyway? How far would the responsibilities of this new department, including the high-profile Transportation Security Administration (TSA), extend? In what way would the newly formed intelligence division of DHS operate? More generally, what role, exactly, would this department actually play—both in the homeland and in its security?

Operational hurdles proved in many ways more tractable, owing in large measure to the fact that a number of the agencies that made up DHS were anything but new—Customs and Border Protection (CBP) traced its active lineage to 1789, the Coast Guard to 1790, the Secret Service to 1865, and the Federal Emergency Management Agency (FEMA) had been signed into law 25 years earlier. These agencies brought with them proud and distinctive cultures, as well as operational maturity with a history of delivering on their missions.

Soon highly visible to all Americans at every airport, border crossing, immigration office, and natural disaster, with its distinctive uniforms, patches, grant-making and regulatory powers, and policy-making authority, DHS rapidly gained clear and widespread brand name recognition—at home and abroad. What it persistently lacked, however, was clear and widespread brand name *understanding*. In other words, DHS had become well known, but not known well. And while its major operational responsibilities reflected longstanding roles and responsibilities of its operating agencies, these operations were now on a much bigger stage, and those efforts were subject to far greater scrutiny than ever before. Indeed, DHS faced the continual challenge of reconciling the deep tensions inherent in its missions: at the borders and in the air, for example, how would it simultaneously work aggressively to keep out people and things that might be dangerous, while at the same time rapidly expedite legitimate trade and travel for a population and country eager to return to "normal"?

Bureaucratic battles over turf, resources, purpose, and primacy were daily trials, especially with the other heavyweights of national security: the Departments of Defense, Justice, and State, as well as the intelligence community. Within just five years of the department's establishment, many policy makers, academics, and politicians were directly questioning the value of DHS. The public's skepticism was more fundamental: Given all this new hassle, has DHS made us safer or not from another terrorist attack on American soil?

DHS had little room to maneuver and even less room to innovate—a harsh reality for this overwhelmingly operational department. Wait times lengthened at border crossings and at airports. The flying public, still only slowly making its way back into the air, recorded every miscue of TSA (the establishment of which was a heroic effort under extraordinary circumstances). Indeed, a thoroughly fussed national security bureaucracy believed that this experiment in homeland security would soon run its course.

But facts and fate are always strong allies, and both were on the side of this new department struggling to establish a clear value proposition and narrative for American security in an uncertain world. The facts reflect the numbers: after 9/11, every major American city and municipality—nearly 40,000 domestic jurisdictions—awakened to the realization that neither the U.S. military nor the intelligence community could protect against determined terrorists operating within the United States. From 2004 onward, billions of dollars in grants from DHS were directed to major urban areas to address the palpable need to strengthen these population centers against such strikes. In addition, hundreds of millions of federal dollars began to flow in the wake of devastating disasters to further shore up community resilience, including rebuilding key infrastructure and further strengthening police, emergency preparedness, and response capabilities. For the 90 percent of the American public that lives within one hour of a major body of water, preparedness against water-borne disasters and the need for on-hand emergency search and rescue tied countless communities to the ongoing work of the Coast Guard and FEMA.

Fate also played its part, as challenges and opportunities emerged immediately and continued seemingly without pause. When Katrina slammed ashore in 2005, events painfully illustrated how vital it had become that the federal government function as a fully capable partner for states and municipalities overwhelmed when disaster strikes. In 2006, a major threat to transatlantic aviation travel was discovered. From 2009 onward, rapid-fire challenges unfolded from nearly every quarter: avian influenza; newly discovered terrorists operating from within the United States; and ongoing vulnerabilities of the global aviation system, exemplified by the so-called underwear bomber (Umar Farouk Abdulmutallab). In 2010, the BP oil spill in the Gulf of Mexico and, later, Hurricane Sandy; tragic shootings in Newtown, Connecticut, and elsewhere; the Boston Marathon bombing; and numerous other crises squarely within the Homeland Security frame of reference drove home the need for Washington to offer a permanent, organized capability to help protect the nation from a wide range of hazards and to respond rapidly with appropriate assistance when they occurred.

In short, tens of thousands of American communities and jurisdictions; hundreds of thousands of state, local, and tribal law enforcement, fire, first responder, and emergency management professionals; and millions of employees across the nation's critical infrastructure (most of which lies in private sector hands) had found their connection to the larger meaning in the powerful idea of homeland security, and they found in DHS a full-time, dedicated federal partner for this "new normal."

As it had rapidly become clear, and certainly in view of the deeply affecting demands of today's world, DHS has become an essential feature on the nation's security landscape. Yet, until we recognize the distinctive culture and approach that characterize homeland security, we will fall short in leveraging the full value of its unique strengths.

Understanding Homeland Security

Effectively leveraging homeland security begins with recognizing how different it truly is from what we usually mean when we say national security—the principal purpose of which is to identify and defend the vital interests of this country against those (usually other countries) who would threaten the United States. The distinctions begin with significant differences in each discipline's fundamental frame of reference and extend to marked differences in culture and operating style.

The traditional approach to national security is strategic; its processes for decision-making are centralized, and its operations are top-driven. National security culture is reflected in the histories and practice of diplomacy, intelligence, and defense. Washington serves as the "national command authority," with the final word in security decisions. National security functions best as a well-organized hierarchy; unity of command serves as a core concept, a premium is placed on readiness to respond, and information is shared on the basis of "need to know."

In contrast, homeland security is best understood as a transactional and operational world where authority and decisions are decentralized, and events are driven from the bottom-up—from the communities, municipalities, and states across the United States. The homeland security culture is reflected in the operations and experience of law enforcement, emergency response, and the domestic politics of American society. In homeland security, Washington functions not as a national command authority, but rather as the federal partner. Homeland security calls on each of us to do our part: to say something if we see something. Operations are not carried out by unifying under a single command, but rather through a far more flexible approach called unity of effort, where the authorities and expertise of multiple jurisdictions mobilize on a common task. In homeland security, a premium is placed on prevention, and important information is exchanged as a duty to share, not withheld unless there is demonstrable "need to know."

Indeed, entire problem sets look different from the two perspectives. Fighting terrorism, for example, illustrates this point. National leaders—indeed, all of us—remain rightly concerned that terrorists are still determined to come to the United States to carry out attacks. U.S. national security efforts, including the very best of our diplomatic, intelligence, and military agencies have worked overtime to find such terrorists and keep them far away from our shores. The homeland security enterprise supports these efforts by mobilizing and deploying its aviation security and border authorities to help us know at the earliest possible moment when malevolent actors may be trying to come to the United States so that the country can take appropriate action.

In contrast, homeland security approaches terrorism with the realization that terrorists are already here. Diplomacy, national intelligence, and military operations must shift to a supporting role to cope with this reality. To fight domestic terrorism, homeland security agencies must lead. When operating to best effect, they open up a two-way exchange with state and local communities to provide multifaceted means to equip domestic law enforcement with information and insights gained from the national security apparatus and, in turn, to draw directly on their knowledge, experience, vigilance, and operations. The combination is a powerful one.

Going Forward

What does the foregoing suggest for how DHS and its role might best mature in its second decade? How should the next administration evolve the domestic effort to prevent terrorism, protect the American homeland (including to ensure the cybersecurity of the nation's critical infrastructure), and build capacity to mitigate and withstand disasters?

Homeland security will provide a platform for the next administration to increase meaningful cooperation with state, local, tribal, and territorial partners, as well as the private sector, while strengthening individual privacy, civil rights, and civil liberties (especially important in the face of the massive collection and use of data by all manner of public and private organizations). DHS should also work more aggressively with state and local partners to provide the public with additional concrete tools (such as the widely adopted "See Something; Say Something" and "Know Before You Go" programs) to underscore the importance of the American people as an essential asset, not obstacle, in the protection of this nation.

Every new administration presents a fresh opportunity to reconsider the alignment between structure and purpose in the federal space. For DHS, two immediate suggestions come to mind. First, integrate Homeland Security Investigations (HSI)—currently part of Immigration and Customs Enforcement (ICE)—with CBP. Approximately 60 percent of HSI's current work directly supports CBP, and these elements should be more tightly integrated in the protection mission. They should be laser-focused on screening, targeting, and leveraging the terabytes of information we have on the global movement of people and goods while providing state-of-the-art protections to privacy, civil rights, and civil liberties.

Second, the next administration should use DHS to elevate preparedness and mitigation to shore up community resilience. The federal government spends nearly twenty times more in post-disaster assistance as it does on mitigation. Such spending is completely out of whack. The federal government should take a much stronger stand on community preparedness—especially for predictable disasters, such as seasonal flooding and severe weather—and FEMA should be empowered and funded to incentivize effective mitigation measures before disaster strikes.

In addition, there are two areas in which the next administration can leverage DHS more effectively with immediate results: to achieve measurably stronger cybersecurity and (perhaps somewhat unexpectedly) to advance U.S. international interests and bolster its foreign policy priorities.

Cybersecurity

To make real progress in cybersecurity, several core issues must be sorted out. First, we must figure out how to architect systems we can trust from components we can't. Second, we must find reliable ways to ensure the integrity of people's information and identity while maintaining the openness of the Internet. Third, we must figure out what role government will play in all of this. What is already clear is that we cannot run cybersecurity as if it were a massive intelligence program or military operation. Nor can we sustain the level of effort necessary over time by treating cyber events as state secrets (secrecy does not scale) nor as serial criminal investigations.

Cybersecurity will improve when every enterprise does its part, and working on problems with distributed responsibilities is the natural environment of homeland security and for DHS. To truly change the game in cybersecurity, enterprises everywhere must adopt basic cyber hygiene. They should clearly establish what is connected to their systems and networks as well as understand which applications are running (or trying to run) on those systems and networks. They should also install systems that limit and control personnel who have administrative privileges and how those privileges are being used, and they should make effective use of automated detection systems that provide alerts on necessary patches or other corrective actions. These measures alone will measurably reduce vulnerability to 80-90 percent of known problems today. DHS should be charged with working with industry leaders and the insurance industry to incentivize and promulgate this basic standard of due care. The February 2016 report of California's Office of the Attorney General offers one demonstration of the effort described here.

In emphasizing the importance of basic cyber hygiene, the next administration should underscore how the national security and homeland security teams can improve the way they work together to support widespread execution of these foundational protective cyber measures with essential information sharing and innovation to help enterprises adapt to the changing threat landscape.

The International Reach of Homeland Security

The next administration should also recognize and leverage the unique role and value that homeland security and DHS have developed internationally over the past decade. This role for DHS has emerged as officials from interior and public safety ministries across the globe (including, notably, the EU, India, and China) have sought the department's expertise in border operations, immigration, currency integrity, disaster response, and cybersecurity, among other areas. Expanded dramatically in the early years of the Obama administration, this international network of domestic and home ministries has created openings and extended relationships previously unavailable to Washington and has deeply enriched American engagement with governments across the world at a critical time.

Homeland security fits well alongside the U.S. national security architecture, which remains second to none. Yet, to be blunt, without the homeland security dimension, the national security agencies and processes simply cannot do all that needs doing to protect the American homeland or ensure the resilience of the American people. In short, no examination of the U.S. national security architecture today would be complete without considering the concepts, strategies, and operations of homeland security. And while the homeland security enterprise remains very much a work in progress, its contribution can only be fully realized when perceived clearly through its own lens, as well as respected and valued on its own terms.

In the end, the whole point of homeland security is to help create a safe, secure, and resilient place where the American way of life can thrive. Homeland security reveals the simple truth that the success of this task will depend as much on each of us as it will on us all.

Jane Holl Lute serves in the United Nations as Special Coordinator to improve the Organisation's response to sexual exploitation and abuse and concurrently as the Special Adviser to the Secretary-General on the relocation of Camp Hurriya residents outside of Iraq. Prior to re-joining the UN, Dr. Lute served as the Chief Executive Officer at the Center for Internet Security (CIS), an independent, not-for-profit organization established to measurably strengthening the cybersecurity posture of public and private sector enterprises. From 2009 - 2013, Dr. Lute served as Deputy Secretary for the Department of Homeland Security (DHS), functioning as the Department's chief operating officer. From 2003-2007, Dr. Lute served as Assistant Secretary-General for peacekeeping, responsible for comprehensive on-the-ground support to UN peace operations worldwide, and from 2007-2008 she established and led the Department of Field Support. Dr. Lute also served as Assistant Secretary-General for Peacebuilding, responsible for coordinating efforts on behalf of the Secretary-General to build sustainable peace in countries emerging from violent conflict. Previously, she was executive vice-president and chief operating officer of the United Nations Foundation and the Better World Fund and as executive director of the Carnegie Commission on Preventing Deadly Conflict, a global initiative that pioneered the international movement for conflict prevention. Dr. Lute served on the National Security Council staff under both President George H.W. Bush and President William Jefferson Clinton and had a distinguished career in the United States Army. She has a Ph.D. in political science from Stanford University and J.D. from Georgetown University.

Part **4**

MODERNIZING AMERICA'S NATIONAL SECURITY
TOOLS

CHAPTER 11

What Makes the Third Offset Strategy So Important?

James Cartwright
Center for Strategic & International Studies

CHAPTER 12

Prospects for the Third Offset Strategy

Dov S. Zakheim
CNA

CHAPTER 13

War by Other Means:
Geoeconomics and Statecraft
America's Geoeconomic Policy Deficit

Robert D. Blackwill and Jennifer M. Harris
Council on Foreign Relations

CHAPTER 14

Organizational Agility in Defense and National Security
Elephants Learning to Dance

John Dowdy and Kirk Rieckhoff
McKinsey & Company

"The need for a third offset strategy is compelling. The technical innovation to support the desired attributes that underpin this strategy appear to address the key risk factors with significant upside potential."

—JAMES CARTWRIGHT

What Makes the Third Offset Strategy So Important?

James Cartwright
Harold Brown Chair in Defense Policy Studies
Center for Strategic and International Studies

The basic premise of an offset strategy is to expand the battle space and create decisive operational advantage. This is accomplished through the integration of effective organizational, operational, and technical constructs. Historically, these organizational and operational alternatives gain decisive advantage through advances in communications (e.g., moving from smoke, bugles, and flags to radios and, today, networks). The doctrinal constructs that underpin these fundamental shifts are the glue that defines how organizations are employed in operational activities and which technologies generate the greatest leverage in the battle space. We generally acknowledge four of these doctrinal constructs, three of which are associated with modern-day warfare, all of which build on each other in every iteration. The three modern-day constructs are mass, maneuver, and swarm.

Mass reflects the creation of hierarchical formations, stacked in place and attacking in waves. Maneuver reflects synchronized, three-domain operations, whose mobility increases the battle space and employs flanking and surprise to disrupt and penetrate enemy formations. Swarm is the latest instantiation, which employs mass and maneuver through disaggregated, coherent, and autonomous units, exerting a constant probing pressure across six domains. This employs speed, agility, and lethality across vast expanses to converge on an adversary.

Why Create a Third Offset Strategy Now?

The National Intelligence Council's (NIC) Alternate Worlds assessment identified ten megatrends, six of which were considered possible game changers. These trends are listed below and paint a future in which combat operations are increasing in likelihood, lethality, and geographic dispersion.

Mega trends identified in the NIC's Alternate Worlds assessment:

1. The Role of the United States*
2. Crisis-prone Global Economy*
3. Governance Gap*
4. Potential for Increased Conflict*
5. Wider Scope of Regional Instability*
6. Impact of New Technologies*
7. Individual Empowerment
8. Diffusion of Power
9. Demographic Patterns
10. Nexus of Food, Water, Energy

Considered game changers by the NIC

The National Defense Panel (NDP) reviewed the current relevant national security documents and highlighted ten risks for which there is a strategy and resource mismatch; risks were possible, if not likely.

Risks identified by the NDP assessment of the Quadrennial Defense Review (QDR):

1. Ability to address U.S. vital interests informed by adversary capabilities
2. Ability to provide actionable knowledge
3. Availability constructs that deter adversary adventurism
4. The amount of risk we can retire based on what the American people are willing to pay
5. The point at which the trade of capacity for quality fails and why
6. Resource implications and opportunity costs of reconstituting the Strategic Triad in kind
7. Strategy implications of the pivot to Asia
8. A contested space domain
9. A contested cyber domain
10. Defense of the homeland

Based on these assessments, and many other similar findings, U.S. combat arms' advantage is eroding. The costs associated with continued bottom-up incremental improvements cannot sustain decisive operational advantage. Top-down change is necessary to reestablish decisive operational advantage (i.e., the third offset strategy).

A sub-panel for the NDP identified attributes for evaluating high-leverage technologies that could support this new third offset strategy approach. Given the early stages of implementing a doctrinal swarm strategy, the group sought to define its key tenants: the ability to command, control, and move forces and/or effects against an adversary across six domains, synchronized to create constant, probing pressure in order to penetrate, disrupt, and destroy an adversary's will. In generating metrics, effects, and capabilities that created leverage in support of the strategy they identified, the sub-panel members identified four swarm-enabling vectors against which to apply technology:

1. Time and Communications
   a. Coherent sensing
   b. Resilient communications

2. Battle Space
   a. Mobility of command, control, and effects across six domains:
      i. Air
      ii. Land
      iii. Sea
      iv. Space
      v. Cyberspace
      vi. Time
   b. Automation and robotics
   c. Hypersonics—Mach 20 and greater
   d. Directed energy
   e. Cyber
   f. Electronic warfare

3. Combat Load (the number and type of weapons per entity in the battle space)
   a. Agility to address the planned and unplanned adversary actions
   b. The virtual ability to repurpose platforms, delivery systems, and weapons in near-real time
   c. Electric propulsion (e.g., rail gun)

    d. Graduated effects (influence to destruction)

        i. Directed energy

        ii. Cyber

4. Organization

    a. Man-machine partnering (efficient task distribution)

    b. Man-machine cognitive interfaces

    c. Automation and robotics

In generating these focus technologies, there are numerous opportunities and potential game changers in the making, for which we are truly advantaged. This set represents the best forecast for prioritized development of technologies that demonstrate 10x leverage over current capabilities, and to further discriminate, were estimated to generate greater than $10 billion in offset leverage. While the vectors are but a forecast of potential, as attributes they highly correlate with the risk factors and desired end states of the strategy.

The need for a third offset strategy is compelling. The technical innovation to support the desired attributes that underpin this strategy appear to address the key risk factors with significant upside potential. Historically, changes of this magnitude require three to four demographic generations within the armed forces. Sustaining leadership focus and advocacy is likely the highest risk to success.

James Cartwright currently serves as the inaugural holder of the Harold Brown Chair in Defense Policy Studies for the Center for Strategic & International Studies. In addition, he serves as a member of The Raytheon Company Board of Directors, a Harvard Belfer Center Senior Fellow, a defense consultant for ABC News, and a member of the Board of Governors for Wesley Theological Seminary. General Cartwright retired from active duty on 1 September 2011, after 40 years of service in the United States Marine Corps. General Cartwright served as Commander, U.S. Strategic Command, before being nominated and appointed as the 8th Vice Chairman of the Joint Chiefs of Staff. General Cartwright served his four-year tenure as Vice Chairman across two Presidential administrations. He became widely recognized for his technical acumen, vision of future national security concepts, and keen ability to integrate systems, organizations, and people in ways that encouraged creativity and sparked innovation in the areas of strategic deterrence, nuclear proliferation, missile defense, cyber security, and adaptive acquisition processes. Born in Rockford, IL, he attended the University of Iowa and was commissioned a Second Lieutenant of the Marines in 1971. He was both a Naval Flight Officer and Naval Aviator, who flew the F-4 Phantom, OA-4 Skyhawk, and F/A-18 Hornet. General Cartwright is also an advisor for several corporate entities involved in global management consulting; technology services and program solutions; predictive and Big Data Analytics; and advanced systems engineering, integration, and decision-support services. He is a member of the Aspen Strategy Group.

"Once again, America could find itself facing off against a highly capable, technologically advanced adversary. What is less clear is whether the third offset can truly compensate for the ongoing reductions in force structure."

—DOV S. ZAKHEIM

Prospects for the Third Offset Strategy

Dov S. Zakheim
Senior Fellow
CNA

Since the end of World War II, the United States has supported its deterrent posture and maintained military superiority by virtue of its commanding technological lead over all adversaries and competitors. In essence, it has emphasized quality—the quality of its forces, its systems, its support and logistics—over quantity, the raw numbers of weapons and weapons systems that its rivals could field. Secretary of Defense Chuck Hagel and then his successor Secretary Ash Carter, and their deputy, Bob Work, have rightly recognized that America is in danger of losing its technological edge as a result of the worldwide spread of commercial technology that is, or could become, available to rivals and potential enemies. As a result, the Department of Defense (DoD) is pursuing a wide-ranging innovation agenda, encapsulating initiatives focused on attracting and retaining talent and innovative leadership, and on advances in technologies, war gaming, operational concepts, and business practices.

Subsumed within the innovation agenda is what Carter and Work have termed the "third offset strategy." The strategy is termed the "third offset" because it is meant to emulate two previous offset strategies that enabled the United States to rely on the quality of its force posture rather than its quantity. The so-called "first offset" strategy was implemented in the aftermath of both the huge post-World War II drawdown and the Korean War. Faced with the overwhelming numbers of Warsaw Pact forces in Eastern Europe and the Soviet Union, the Eisenhower administration resorted to a strategy of massive nuclear retaliation designed to deter the Pact's forces while avoiding the major expenditures that would have been required to match them quantitatively. The "second offset" took place in the mid-1970s, subsequent to the post-Vietnam drawdown, where once again, the United States relied on cutting-edge technological superiority, in this case for its conventional forces, in order to offset the ongoing numerical superiority of Warsaw Pact force posture in Europe. Thus the "third offset" is simply a continuation of what has been a key aspect of American military strategy for the past six-and-a-half decades, namely, to strengthen deterrence by means of technological superiority.

As has been widely advertised, the third offset strategy exploits advances in artificial intelligence and autonomous systems with a focus on six major areas:

- accelerated research on anti-area/access denial (A2/AD) technologies
- accelerated research on guided munitions
- accelerated research on addressing submarine and other undersea warfare challenges
- human-machine collaboration and teaming
- cyber and electronic warfare
- war gaming and the testing of operational concepts

To support these efforts, the DoD has allocated $18 billion in the Future Years Defense Program, with about $6 billion devoted to classified programs and an initial $3.5 billion included in its fiscal year (FY) 2017 budget. In addition, the DoD is allocating $1 billion to the Strategic Capabilities Office for offset-related activities. This office was created in 2012 to repurpose existing weapons for asymmetric advantage, and it has already managed and fielded over twenty projects. Finally, as part of the strategy, the DoD has requested $45 million in FY 2017 funds for the Defense Innovation Unit Experimental, commonly known as DIUx, whose first office was established in Mountain View, California, to draw upon and incorporate new technologies developed in Silicon Valley. To get DIUx started, the DoD reallocated approximately $20 million from the FY 2016 budget. In July 2016, Secretary Carter opened a second office, located in Cambridge, Massachusetts, near MIT, to tap high-tech advances emerging along the Route 128 corridor, and in mid-September, he opened what he termed a "presence" in Austin, in the heart of the "Silicon Hills" of central Texas. In contrast to the two offices that DIUx currently maintains, the DoD will have DIUx personnel working part-time at Capitol Factory, an Austin-based high-tech incubator, and will also work closely with the University of Texas system, led by retired Admiral William McRaven.

The goal of maintaining America's technological edge in the military domain is certainly a worthy enterprise. Once again, America could find itself facing off against a highly capable, technologically advanced adversary. What is less clear is whether the third offset can truly compensate for the ongoing reductions in force structure. America is facing a renewed challenge from Russia, ongoing friction with China, a long-term commitment to Afghanistan, and a Middle East that continues to demand intensive American military engagement. Lanchester's Law, which argues in effect that quantity has a quality all its own, may not be as applicable as it once was. Nevertheless, technology cannot fully compensate for the depth and worldwide breadth of demands on and for American military forces. In other words, the third offset may not be an offset at all if force levels continue to be reduced. Instead, it is arguable that a new offset strategy can only be viable if it is coupled with an effort to maintain or even increase current force levels.

The Third Offset Strategy and R&D Budgets

Although the DoD has widely publicized its third offset strategy, many questions remain about its character and prospects. To begin with, the strategy appears to involve a redirection of resources rather than any significant increase in funding per se. The DoD's total research and development budget request for FY 2017 amounted to $71.8 billion, less than $3 billion—or only 1.8 percent—more in real terms than was approved the previous fiscal year. Indeed, although this year's funding level exceeds each of those of the past four fiscal years, it represents growth from a low baseline; research and development had suffered from severe spending reductions during those years.

The downward trend in spending began in FY 2012, when the budget dropped by 7.5 percent in real terms from that of the preceding fiscal year. It then dropped by another 13.2 percent in FY 2013. FY 2017 represents the second year of a slow recovery from a base of just under $66 billion in FY 2015; when measured in constant dollars, the FY 2017 level falls short of R&D spending in each fiscal year from 2003-2012.

This year's request therefore does not constitute a resurgence in spending on research and development, the heart of any technologically driven offset strategy. For the offset strategy to succeed, the R&D budget must grow by larger percentages in future fiscal years. In fact, total R&D spending is projected once again to decline in FY 2019. This hardly represents the makings of a viable offset strategy.

"Black Programs" and Funding for Cyber Warfare

The DoD has for decades pursued the development of classified, or in common parlance "black," programs that are shielded from public scrutiny until they are virtually ready for production. For example, the B-2 stealth bomber, under development in the 1970s, was not publicly discussed until 1980. Classified programs cannot be evaluated outside the Office of the Secretary of Defense in terms of their costs, effectiveness, efficiency, or the degree to which they are duplicative, because access to these programs is so heavily restricted.

There are excellent reasons for not revealing the nature of the programs for which $6 billion is being allocated as part of the offset strategy. Still, their opaqueness allows for no way to determine whether the funds for such programs are adequate to the task, are being spent in a most cost-effective manner, and avoid any overlap with current projects.

Similar observations apply to the DoD's plans, as part of the third offset, to spend $1.7 billion on cyber and electronic warfare. The details of cyber warfare in particular tend to be highly classified. While there is more visibility into the amounts of money being spent on cyber programs than on "black programs," there is far less clarity about how successful those programs actually are. Indeed, there continues to be considerable difficulty in determining appropriate output measures for cyber programs that could allow for cost-effectiveness analyses, at least those that might be conducted in the unclassified world and perhaps those in the classified world as well. In effect, the DoD is asking that the classified elements of the offset strategy be taken on faith alone. One can only hope that the monies will be well spent.

The Cultural and Educational Challenge to the Third Offset Strategy

Technological advances require experimentation; attempts to accelerate those advances even more so. Experimentation, by its very definition, calls for risk-taking and a recognition that experiments can and will fail. Yet, experimentation flies in the face of the DoD's bureaucratic culture, which has become increasingly more risk-averse, indeed ossified, over the decades. Fear of failure seems to dominate the acquisition bureaucracy, yet fearlessness is a necessary condition for experimentation and, ultimately, for successful technological advances. The offset strategy implicitly presupposes that the bureaucracy will embrace experimentation and not penalize failure. How such behavior can be encouraged and ultimately modified in accordance with the strategy's urgent timetable remains an open question.

The bureaucracy needs to change in another respect as well. Currently, the DoD is not a sufficiently educated consumer because continuing advanced technological education is not a prerequisite for promotion and leadership within its ranks. The Defense Acquisition University (DAU), which is the primary focal point for the continuing education of many senior acquisition officials, is too heavily oriented toward online programs. These programs may or may not successfully educate those who are taking the DAU's courses. In any event, the DAU is more a vehicle for training than education, and there is simply no substitute for the type of education that students receive at America's great institutes of technology, such as MIT, Rensselaer Polytechnic Institute, Caltech, and the like.

In practice, a civilian member of the defense acquisition corps can advance to the highest ranks without ever taking another course after his or her master's-level degree in physics, computer sciences, engineering, or other technology-related subjects. This hardly creates educated consumers and could well undermine the types of rapid breakthrough advances that the third offset strategy presupposes.

The DoD should impose a far more rigorous requirement for civilians to pursue continuing education in technology-related fields than is currently the case. It should also initiate a program for civilian officials akin to the Secretary of Defense (SecDef) Fellows program, which enables some twenty field-grade officers to spend a year with a commercial firm. In general, these firms are not part of the traditional defense industrial base, rendering the program exceedingly relevant to Secretary Carter's push to reach beyond that base. A requirement for at least one full semester's course load at a leading institute of technology, with another half year in a civilian version of the SecDef Fellows program, could be tied to promotion to the top managerial and deputy managerial positions in the acquisition corps, and certainly to promotion to the Senior Executive Service. In that way, the DoD acquisition bureaucracy could keep up with changes in technology, which are taking place with the speed of Moore's Law, and would be in a position to administer the offset strategy more effectively than is likely to be the case today.

The Strategic Capabilities Office and Accelerated Research

Accelerated research and development is a critical element of the third offset strategy. Yet the DoD is notorious for its slow-moving bureaucracy. In fact, the DoD had to implement a "rapid acquisition" system to get around its own acquisition system! This troublesome reality was a major factor in Secretary Carter's decision to create a Strategic Capabilities Office to exploit existing technologies, especially advanced commercial technology, in novel ways to support military operations—and to field those technologies far more quickly than usual for DoD. As noted, the office was created well before the formulation of the offset strategy, and its activities have now been incorporated into that strategy.

Part of the reason for the bureaucracy's inability to bring projects to the production stage more quickly is its above-noted cautiousness and risk-aversion. But there are other reasons as well. The system has too many review cycles. It requires far too many offices to concur before a project can move forward, what has been termed the "tyranny of consensus." It tolerates too many changes to engineering change proposals (ECPs) during the course of a project's development, adding unnecessary costs and schedule delays. Projects can take years, sometimes decades, to reach completion. As a result, many systems have been terminated well before their anticipated production runs. In some cases, a weapon system has taken so long to develop that it is virtually obsolescent upon its incorporation into the force structure and must be terminated. For example, the Army's Division Air Defense gun, later called the Crusader, took so long to develop that it was out-ranged by its anticipated targets. Schedule delays, even more than cost increases, would completely undermine the intent and potential of the third offset strategy.

In the context of the third offset strategy, the Strategic Capabilities Office's mission is to accelerate DoD's acquisition of AA/AD programs and submarine acoustic and related underwater technologies, among others. Yet it is not at all clear what "acceleration" actually means with respect to these and other ongoing programs incorporated into the offset strategy. Perhaps it means applying the same methods that have underpinned the success of the rapid acquisition policy.

Yet one might question why accelerated efforts were not already launched some time ago, when force levels began to drop. For example, it has been argued that the new Hypervelocity Gun Weapons System, or HGWS, adapts projectiles originally developed for the Navy's electromagnetic rail gun program to artillery systems that have been in the force for some time. Yet, since hypervelocity development, whether for projectiles or weapons, has been ongoing for several years, it is unclear why such adaptation was not contemplated some time ago. After all, adaptation has a long history in the military, with the land-based SM-3 missile a recent example. Similarly, the Navy has spent years developing unmanned undersea vehicles (UUVs) and enhancing submarine acoustics. Presumably it has done so with the utmost urgency, and if not, one might question why the Office of the Secretary did not mandate that it do so.

In any event, for the Strategic Capabilities Office to have any hope of success, the acquisition system may have to be modified more than is currently planned. In addition, radical steps will be necessary to ensure that the acquisition work force is responsive to those changes. And changing the DoD's acquisition culture will pose a far more daunting challenge both for the office and for the strategy it seeks to implement.

The Prospects for DIUx

In many respects, DIUx is the crown jewel of the third offset strategy. The office was created to reach out to the commercial high-tech sector, whose advances have not been fully absorbed by the DoD. With his personal knowledge of developments in Silicon Valley, Secretary of Defense Carter was particularly well-placed to initiate such a path-breaking entity.

To succeed, DIUx will have to find ways to enable the commercial sector to work more closely with DoD than in the past. This is no small matter. Commercial firms are profit-driven. They invest in research in order to get returns when their products reach the market. They seek both to develop a competitive advantage and maintain it during the length of their production runs. They are not averse to selling military wares—Amazon has reportedly designed drones for Indonesia—but are wary of doing business with DoD.

Despite protestations to the contrary, DoD's business practices act as disincentives to working with firms that are outside the defense industrial base. The DoD procurement system is complicated, stove-piped, and over-regulated. Its cost accounting standards require firms to have a second set of financial statements alongside those that comply with generally accepted accounting principles. Its emphasis on lowest price, technically acceptable contracting is the polar opposite of commercial firms' profit-driven practices.

In addition, few of the Department's career acquisition officials have any real experience in the private sector. As a result, even when they do have the opportunity to acquire commercial items in accordance with Federal Acquisition Regulations (FAR Part 12), defense officials default to DoD's traditional contract by negotiation methods (FAR Part 15), with which they are more familiar and therefore more comfortable. It is therefore not surprising that many commercial firms, especially technology leaders, are loath to entangle themselves with DoD's regulations and bureaucracy.

DIUx's initial efforts to overcome the suspicions of commercial firms regarding working with DoD were not very successful. As a result, Secretary Carter announced an overhaul of the office, bringing in new leadership directly from the commercial sector. This was an important step. So too was his creation of the Defense Digital Service, which will bring into DoD technologists from commercial high-tech firms for a short-term tour of duty. Moreover, DIUx can avoid many of the pitfalls and associated paperwork of the acquisition system because, thanks to congressional legislation, DoD has granted DIUx Other Transaction Authority (OTA). Under

OTA, DIUx can enter into transactions other than contracts, grants, or cooperative agreements, and these transactions are not covered by the FAR. Finally, DIUx awards are not subject to audits by the Defense Contract Audit Agency, whose huge backlog has forced companies to hold funds in reserve in case an audit, when it finally takes place, requires the company to return funds to the government.

Clearly, DIUx has been given a number of advantages that to some extent already have enhanced its ability to reach out to the commercial high-tech sector. Still, it will take much work to convince high-tech companies in Silicon Valley and similar research hubs, whether these firms are small start-ups or behemoths whose market capitalization far exceeds those of major defense companies, that it pays to work with DoD. Moreover, it will be easier to change regulations than the culture of the entrenched bureaucracy (which, incidentally, may not mesh well with the temporary imports from the commercial sector), but both are necessary conditions for DoD in general and DIUx in particular to achieve their objectives.

As noted, the DoD has provided DIUx with about $20 million in initial funding and has requested just under $45 million in its FY 2017 budget proposal. In mid-September, when he opened the DIUx office in Austin, Secretary Carter announced that some $65 million in contracts would soon be awarded. These represent $17 million of DIUx funds matched by $51 million provided by the services. In defense budget terms, these are paltry sums. Admittedly, any project that DIUx supports receives matching funds for its sponsoring service, and because of their nature as technology demonstrators, DIUx projects do not require huge investments. For example, acting on behalf of the Navy Special Warfare Command, DIUx awarded $1 million to a small California company for a nine-month project to develop a prototype development of an autonomous tactical airborne drone.

Nevertheless, there are limits to what can be done with $45 million—or even $135 million, assuming the services continue to be willing to co-invest on a 3:1 basis—when the purpose of an operation like DIUx is to tap the nation's innovative capabilities across the range of potential military requirements. Moreover, these funding levels would have to be maintained, if not grow, for perhaps five years if the DIUx experiment is to succeed. Disruptions in funding would render it difficult to sustain cooperation with high-tech innovators.

In some cases, DIUx already has achieved success, with the military directly absorbing the commercial innovations that it has sponsored. Examples include autonomous unmanned sailboats, neuro-stimulation systems, and removable communications devices that can be hidden in one's mouth. In general, however, a successful prototype demonstration would still require a major investment for engineering development and production. Funds for these efforts have yet to be identified, and even if available, the programs themselves would still confront both the schedule and bureaucratic challenges that continue to bedevil the acquisition system.

In particular, even if DIUx successfully orchestrates the sale to the military of high-tech prototypes produced by nontraditional suppliers, these systems may still have to undergo modification, unless military specification, "milspec," requirements are fully waived. Milspec has been the bane of potential foreign supplies to the U.S. military; foreign systems have at times been changed beyond recognition in order to meet specification requirements. For DIUx to succeed in generating DoD acquisition of commercial cutting-edge technologies, encouraging companies to make such technologies available to the military, and ensuring that commercial high-tech products are not so transmogrified that their costs skyrocket and their delivery schedules are seriously delayed, DoD will have to ensure that the military's approach to milspec is fundamentally revised.

Finally, it is important that the DIUx managing partners remain in their positions for a meaningful term. DIUx is caught on the horns of a dilemma: if its leaders hold their jobs for too long, they will lose the edge that keeps them current with the most dynamic elements of U.S. high technology. On the other hand, too frequent changes of leadership will undermine organizational efficiency and effectiveness. A term of not less than two years, but not more than three, appears appropriate.

DIUx, High-Tech, and the Reserves

As part of his DIUx initiative, Secretary Carter created a Joint Reserve Element, which, as he noted at the opening of the Austin "presence," "enables DIUx to leverage the capabilities and connections of our citizen soldiers who serve as tech industry leaders when they're not on duty for us in DoD." The Element is led by Doug Beck, a Naval reserve commander, who in civilian life reports to Tim Cook, Apple's CEO, and also has advised senior military leaders as a member of the Chief of Naval Operations Executive Panel. In his remarks in Austin, Carter announced that the Element would expand its presence to include the Texas high-tech center and would draw upon Guard and Reserve members who are innovators in their civilian lives. These personnel will help DIUx develop relationships with people in industry and academia who are developing the innovative technologies that could have a major impact on warfighter capabilities.

Until now, the military has not had a consistent policy of assigning high-tech experts, whether corporate leaders or staff technologists, to related fields—such as cyber or defense research—while serving in their capacity in the Reserves. All too often, a cyber expert or a CEO of a cutting-edge high-tech firm will find him or herself driving trucks or working in the ship's engine room when he or she dons the uniform. The significance of Secretary Carter's initiative therefore extends well beyond DIUx. It should serve as both a model for, and a spur to, the services to create military occupational specialties that relate directly to the high-tech capabilities of their Reserve personnel.

What Are the Trade-Offs?

Underpinning the third offset strategy is the premise that some research and development and/or procurement programs previously included in the defense baseline can be slowed, or even terminated. Many of these programs address shorter-term concerns; the offset strategy is meant for the medium-to-long term; that is, its effects will be felt by 2020 and beyond. And, as noted above, the strategy is meant to serve as an offset in another sense, namely, to compensate for shrinking force levels, particularly those of land forces.

The reordering of priorities begs the question of whether it makes sense to sacrifice the near for the longer term, given the speed with which threats can materialize, as the rapid growth of ISIS clearly demonstrates. While the sequester will be a source of downward pressure on the budget for several more years, Congress has demonstrated ways to circumvent its most dire effects. A new budget deal could be struck; or the Overseas Contingency Account could be increased. In both cases, DoD could sustain its offset strategy while preserving many programs that the strategy currently is anticipated to supersede.

Sustainability Is Critical

Secretary Carter and Deputy Secretary Work should be commended for their formulation of a new offset strategy geared to the evolving international environment and for their determination to push the strategy along several fronts. These include, most notably, accelerating research and development programs that for whatever reason have not matured as quickly as was possible; reaching out to the commercial sector to inject innovation and new technologies into the current defense base; and hiring officials from that sector who understand how to introduce those technologies with far greater rapidity than has been the case with DoD's usual processes.

A new administration will take office in January 2017, however, and with it a potential change of leadership within the DoD. It is crucial that the third offset strategy be seen as extending over the life of several administrations and be treated as the strategy of "containment" once was, namely, as a bipartisan strategy that underwent relatively minor modifications over a period of more than half a century.

The new secretary of defense and his or her deputy must assign the new offset strategy the same priority that it has received from the current incumbents of those offices. Indeed, they should build upon the foundation that Secretary Carter and Deputy Secretary Work have constructed. They should continue to improve the speed with which systems are developed and acquired. They should focus on transforming the acquisition corps into an educated consumer that benefits from, and draws upon, a rigorous program of continuing education. They should maintain, if not increase, the turnaround in research and development spending that began in FY 2016 and extend it beyond FY 2018. Finally, they should consider with the utmost care whether the third offset strategy, as deserving of priority as it is, should be implemented at the expense of near-term programs. For these programs may continue to be urgently required in an international environment that has become increasingly unstable and that continues to call upon American military capabilities more in the near future.

Dov S. Zakheim is Senior Fellow at CNA and Senior Advisor at the Center for Strategic and International Studies. From 2001 to 2004, he was Under Secretary of Defense (Comptroller) and Chief Financial Officer for the Department of Defense; from 2002-2004, he also was DOD's coordinator of civilian programs in Afghanistan. From 1985 until 1987, Dr. Zakheim was Deputy Under Secretary of Defense for Planning and Resources. Dr. Zakheim has served on numerous government, corporate, non-profit, and charitable boards, including the Congressionally-mandated Commission on Wartime Contracting in Iraq and Afghanistan and the Military Compensation and Retirement Modernization Commission. He currently is a member of the Chief of Naval Operations Executive Panel, the Council on Foreign Relations, the Royal Institute of International Affairs/Chatham House (UK), and the Defense Business Board, which he helped to establish. He is a Fellow of the Royal Swedish Academy of War Sciences and a member of the Aspen Strategy Group. A 1970 graduate of Columbia University with a B.A., summa cum laude, Dr. Zakheim also studied at the London School of Economics. He holds a doctorate in economics and politics at St. Antony's College, University of Oxford. The author of numerous articles, monographs, and books, Dr. Zakheim lectures and provides media commentary on national security issues domestically and internationally. He blogs on Foreign Policy/Shadow Government and The National Interest. He is the recipient of numerous awards for his government, professional, and civic work, including the Defense Department's highest civilian award in 1986, 1987, and 2004.

"In ignoring the ever-greater role of geoeconomics in the international system, the United States squanders opportunities and dilutes its own foreign policy outcomes. It weakens the confidence of America's Asian and European allies."

—ROBERT D. BLACKWILL AND JENNIFER M. HARRIS

War by Other Means:
Geoeconomics and Statecraft[1]

Robert D. Blackwill
Henry A. Kissinger Senior Fellow for U.S. Foreign Policy
Council on Foreign Relations

Jennifer M. Harris[2]
Senior Fellow
Council on Foreign Relations

America's Geoeconomic Policy Deficit

Despite having the most powerful economy on earth, the United States too often reaches for the gun instead of the purse in its international conduct. America has hardly outgrown its need for military force, which will remain a central component of U.S. foreign policy. But Washington in the past several decades has increasingly forgotten a tradition that stretches back to the founding of the nation—the systematic use of economic instruments to accomplish geopolitical objectives, what we in this book term geoeconomics. This large-scale failure of collective strategic memory denies Washington potent tools to accomplish its foreign policy objectives.

To compound matters, as economic techniques of statecraft have become a lost art in the United States, the rest of the world has moved in the opposite direction. Russia, China, and others now routinely look to geoeconomic means, often as a first resort, and often to undermine American power and influence. In ignoring the ever-greater role of geoeconomics in the international system, the United States squanders opportunities and dilutes its own foreign policy outcomes. It weakens the confidence of America's Asian and European allies. It encourages China to coerce its neighbors and lessens their ability to resist. It gives China free rein in vulnerable African and

---

1 This chapter is an adaptation of excerpts from *War by Other Means: Geoeconomics and Statecraft* by Robert D. Blackwill and Jennifer M. Harris, Cambridge, Mass.: The Belknap Press of Harvard University Press, Copyright © 2016 by Robert D. Blackwell and Jennifer M. Harris.

2 Robert D. Blackwill is Henry A. Kissinger Senior Fellow for U.S. Foreign Policy at the Council on Foreign Relations. Jennifer M. Harris is a Senior Fellow at the Council on Foreign Relations.

Latin American nations. It allows Russia to bend much of the former Soviet space to its will without serious answer from the United States. It reduces U.S. influence in friendly Arab capitals. It insufficiently acknowledges the economic roots of much of Islamic radicalism. These costs weigh on specific U.S. policy aims. But they also risk accumulating over time into a structural disadvantage that Washington may find hard to reverse. In short, the global geoeconomic playing field is now sharply tilting against the United States, and unless this is corrected, the price in blood and treasure for the United States will only grow.

Should Washington send lethal weapons to Ukraine? Should the North Atlantic Treaty Organization (NATO) reestablish a permanent presence in Eastern Europe? Should the United States directly arm the Iraqi Kurds in the fight against the Islamic State of Iraq and al-Sham (ISIS)? Should it intervene militarily in the Syrian civil war? Should America deploy boots on the ground in Iraq? Was an attack on Iran's nuclear facilities really an option for President Obama? What should be the military components of the Obama administration's pivot toward Asia? How many U.S. combat forces should remain in Afghanistan over the long term?

In the current era and across the political spectrum, the United States instinctively debates the application of military instruments to address all of these complex challenges. There is no comparable discussion in Washington of returning Ukraine to economic viability as a way to check Vladimir Putin's designs for a Novorossiya, or "New Russia"; of prioritizing economic and financial denial strategies in the fight against ISIS; of making reform of the Egyptian economy a primary U.S. foreign policy objective; of strengthening Jordan to withstand the effects of the Syrian conflict; of building a Middle East coalition to blunt the economic transmission lines Iran relies upon to project influence in the region; of mounting a major, patient effort to bolster the faltering Afghan economy, a prerequisite for defeating the Taliban over the long run; of building into the Trans-Pacific Partnership agreement or into the Asia pivot more broadly, defenses to help U.S. allies steel themselves against economic bullying from China.

The decline of geoeconomics in American foreign policy making in recent decades proves to be a complicated story, with lots of variables, sub-plots, and nuances. But the short version is a combination of neglect and resistance. American economists tend to resist putting economic policies to work for geopolitical purposes, in part because the notion of subjugating economics in this way challenges some of their deepest disciplinary assumptions. As Michael Mandelbaum put it in his latest book, "The heart of politics is power; the aim of economics is wealth. Power is inherently limited. The quest for power is therefore competitive. It is a 'zero-sum game' ... Wealth, by contrast, is limitless, which makes economics a 'positive-sum game.'"[1] Because many U.S. economists and economic policy makers tend to see the world through this positive-sum logic and have little appreciation for the realities of power competition among nations, they tend to be skeptical of using economic policies to strengthen America's power projection vis-à-vis its state competitors.

The notion has also encountered ambivalence from foreign policy strategists. Although they are steeped in traditional geopolitics and are not averse to viewing economic instruments of statecraft within a zero-sum logic, most strategists fail to recognize the power and potential of economics and finance as instruments of national purpose.

Thus embraced by neither most economists nor most foreign policy strategists, the use of economic and financial instruments as tools of statecraft has become an orphaned subject. For a time, it seemed of no great consequence. In the years following the Cold War, the United States faced no serious geopolitical rival, no real struggle for international influence or in the contest of ideas. Liberal economic consensus pervaded. And as it did, what began as a set of liberal economic prescriptions aimed at limiting the rightful role of government in the market morphed over time into a doctrinal unwillingness to accept economics as subject to geopolitical choices and influence. Thus, certain liberal economic policy prescriptions, such as trade liberalization, that found favor initially at least in part because they were seen as advantageous to U.S. foreign policy objectives came over time to be justified predominantly on the internal logic of laissez-faire liberalism, not on the basis of (perhaps even in spite of) U.S. geopolitical grounds. "A policy of free trade logically can—and should—be viewed as a technique of economic statecraft," David Baldwin, international relations theorist at Columbia University, once put it.[2] "This is not to say, however, that the economic doctrine of laissez faire liberalism [has been] conducive to viewing free trade in this way, at least not in the 20th century."[3]

But now, of course, the so-called end of history has itself come to an end.[4] The United States once again finds itself competing for global influence and ideas— and doing so alongside a set of states, many of them rising powers, that pledge no particular allegiance to these same liberal economic understandings, do not make any such disciplinary divides between geopolitics and economics in their own policy making, and are thoroughly comfortable with harnessing economic tools to work their strategic will in the world. The result is a set of challenges for which the current tools of U.S. statecraft, dominated by traditional political-military might, are uniquely unsuited. In short, the time has come for America's foreign policy and national security establishment to systematically rethink some of its most basic premises, including the composition of power itself. A new way of addressing U.S. national interests and power must aim for a foreign policy suited to a world in which economic concerns often—but obviously not always—trump traditional military ones.

Crafting U.S. Geoeconomic Policies

American geoeconomic potential is inherently promising. But Washington must first face a set of questions about the country's overall comfort level with restoring geoeconomics as a more considered part of its foreign policy. Skeptics will argue that more straightforward attempts to link economic and geopolitical agendas will result in a race to the bottom. But the alternative cannot be to do nothing. In any case, the surest means of avoiding such a downward spiral may be to recognize what the United States is now dealing with: a set of states thoroughly comfortable employing most of the tools of geoeconomics to advance state power and geopolitical goals, often in ways that undermine U.S. national interests and chip away at the U.S.-led rules-based economic order.

Again, for U.S. policy makers, to recognize this is not to advocate necessarily a response in kind. On the contrary, America's long-term prosperity and security are ultimately staked upon what Benn Steil and Robert Litan call "a liberal, rules-based international economic and political order to which people around the globe aspire to be attached ... An enlightened American financial statecraft will always be consistent with this principle."[5] It is, though, to advocate a different kind of policy debate, one where all sides begin from a clear geopolitical objective and where geoeconomic proposals are measured against that objective and in the context of viable alternatives. In extreme instances the alternative may be war. Where this is the case, U.S. officials need to ensure more appropriate standards of debate and comparison in weighing various options and their relative trade-offs.

To be sure, the United States should not re-create an office focused on "economic warfare." But the underlying lesson remains valid. For example, coming to terms with the uncomfortable reality that markets represented an unavoidable front in the war on terror was not easy.[6] But once this point won reluctant interagency acceptance following 9/11, the U.S. government launched a range of initiatives that have since drawn wide praise for their effectiveness in targeting terrorism without sacrificing American lives and economic liberties.[7] Paradigm-shifting approaches and tools have often seemed impossible or sacrilegious when they were first introduced, from convincing NATO allies to adopt nuclear "flexible response" at the height of the Cold War to proceeding with new forms of sanctions (targeting energy and central banking, for example). But after a hard-fought battle for acceptance, these have proven crucial in addressing the nuclear ambitions of North Korea and Iran.

In short, vital and very important U.S. national interests are again at stake in how we wage a very different sort of campaign. This time the goal is to shape the behavior of states that wield substantial economic and financial muscle and are in some ways, though not in others, using this leverage to pursue policies that could be damaging to U.S. national interests. As one market observer summarized the task facing policy makers, "It's [about] re-writing the rules of diplomacy to better engage" in a world where influence "is determined by economic power."[8] The United States has such geoeconomic assets. The abiding question is how effectively it will use them.

What, as a practical matter, would such a geoeconomic-centric U.S. foreign policy agenda specifically entail? What would it require? We believe it would be animated by the following presidential and congressional vision: U.S. foreign policy must be reshaped to address a world in which economic concerns often outweigh traditional military imperatives and where geoeconomic approaches are often the surest means of advancing American national interests. It must also systematically address the domestic economic sources of American power projection.

There will inevitably be times where our security or our democratic values lead us to act abroad. We will always face international threats. But returning geoeconomics to the helm of U.S. foreign policy means that, for these cases and indeed every foreign policy decision we make, we must ask three questions: How does this affect America's economic position in the world? How can we use geoeconomic tools to advance our strategic interests? And how can we shape emerging economic trends to produce geopolitical results beneficial to the United States, to our allies and friends, and to a rules-based global order?

U.S. Foreign Policy in an Age of Geoeconomics: A Twenty-Point Agenda

Next comes the difficult task of translating this vision into concrete lines of action. We offer twenty specific policy prescriptions—by no means an exhaustive list, but taken together, they would amount to a meaningful and self-reinforcing improvement in U.S. geoeconomic performance.

POLICY PRESCRIPTION 1

Nothing would better promote America's geoeconomic agenda and strategic future than robust economic growth in the United States.[9]

Economists are a contentious lot, but there is a wide, bipartisan consensus—further backed by the IMF—that U.S. growth over the next decade will require increased public and private investment in the near term, and a solution to the U.S. entitlement pressures over the longer term.[10] Both at the federal level and in most states, the United States is spending less on education in 2015 than before the 2008–2009 recession—amounting in some cases to a 10 percent drop in spending per child. And the Congressional Budget Office assesses that federal infrastructure spending is roughly 60 percent of what is needed to maintain current economic growth rates. By contrast, according to the U.S. Chamber of Commerce, citing economic analysis by the University of Maryland, a "targeted and long-term increase in public infrastructure investments from all public and private sources over the next 15 years would increase jobs by almost 1.3 million at the onset of an initial boost, and grow real GDP 1.3% by 2020 and 2.9% by 2030."[11]

POLICY PRESCRIPTION 2

The president must speak to geoeconomic policy.

The next president should lay out an affirmative vision for a geoeconomic-centered foreign policy—backed by a mandate for the changes, big and small, it will require of her or his foreign policy establishment. Without presidential geoeconomic leadership, Pavlovian political-military responses are likely to most often carry the day in Washington, and thus drive the bureaucratic responses to America's external challenges.

POLICY PRESCRIPTION 3

The leadership of the Congress should schedule a comprehensive set of hearings on the potential of the United States to use economic tools to further U.S. geopolitical objectives.

Much of the needed U.S. geoeconomic agenda cannot be implemented without congressional approval. The Constitution gives Congress the preeminent role in U.S. trade policy, yet the last significant congressional overhaul came in the Trade Act of 1984. After thirty years, it is time for a broader legislative overhaul of the current legislative authorities governing U.S. trade policy.

POLICY PRESCRIPTION 4

Funds should be shifted from the Pentagon to be used to promote U.S. national interests through geoeconomic instruments.

The administration's State Department budget request for fiscal year 2016 was $50.3 billion, while the Department of Defense's total FY16 request was $585.2 billion.[12] The State Department figure is 8.6 percent of the Defense Department's request, a ratio that is incompatible with an era of geoeconomic power projection.

POLICY PRESCRIPTION 5

Develop a more concerted understanding of geoeconomics across all executive branch agencies with responsibilities in U.S. foreign policy and national security.

In order to discern when geoeconomics is at work and how it matters for U.S. foreign policy, the U.S. government first needs a common understanding of what geoeconomics is.

POLICY PRESCRIPTION 6

Pass TPP Round 1.

Geopolitical strategy by the United States in Asia cannot succeed without delivering on TPP Round 1, bringing a "comprehensive, high-standards regional trade agreement" to the region.[13] Even though TPP began as a straightforward exercise in liberalizing trade barriers, its geopolitical stakes largely brought in as after-the-fact marketing to win the domestic support needed for its passage in Congress are now real, and were made all the more so by the Obama administration's repeated emphasis.

POLICY PRESCRIPTION 7

Conclude the TTIP agreement with America's European allies.

Nothing else will so further transatlantic geoeconomic prospects—especially if both sides seek to make this a trade agreement that prioritizes geoeconomic aims in its design choices.

POLICY PRESCRIPTION 8

Reboot U.S. alliances for geoeconomic action focused as intensely on shared geoeconomic as on political and military challenges.

For a decade or more, America's economic relationships with many of its closest allies have lagged behind security cooperation. To push Europe to take responsibility for its core security interests, Congress, as part of reauthorizing NATO budgets, should require the secretary of state to certify that the EU has made substantial progress toward diversifying its energy supplies and building in greater resilience to threatened shutoffs—always, of course, with a presidential waiver. The same goes for our treaty allies in Asia. Washington should lead collective negative responses to economic coercion in the region.

POLICY PRESCRIPTION 9

Construct a geoeconomic policy to deal with China over the long term.

America's economic pivot to the Asia-Pacific has lagged behind our diplomatic and military investments. But more than any other region, economics is the coin of the realm in Asia. As we now work out the content of the rebalancing, our strategy must change to reflect this basic reality. To help give teeth to the current principles for resolving the region's territorial disputes, the United States should build on recent warnings against the use of force, and make clear to Beijing that economic coercion, too, will have negative consequences. The United States should work to fortify countries, from Japan to India, against economic coercion—identifying their leading vulnerabilities and assisting with resiliency and diversification efforts to plug these exposures, as well as developing a policy across U.S. treaty allies in the region to ensure that if one ally suffers economic coercion, another doesn't take advantage by filling in behind.

POLICY PRESCRIPTION 10

In another aspect of rebalancing to Asia, the United States should make geoeconomic investments in India's emergence as a Pacific power.

With so much staked on an India that is growing economically and engaged regionally, supporting India in its bid for greater multilateral clout—backing New Delhi in its long-running desire to join the Asia-Pacific Economic Cooperation (APEC), for instance—would seem a minimum ante for the United States.

POLICY PRESCRIPTION 11

Construct a geoeconomic policy to deal with Russia over the long term.

This includes working closely with allies, toughening the U.S. posture on backfilling economic voids created by sanctions, reducing Europe's dependence on Russian oil and gas, increasing economic support for Russia's neighbors in former Soviet space (including ramping up support for Western private investment as an alternative to Russian and Chinese state-led investment, an alternative that many Central Asian and Eastern European leaders are desperately seeking precisely for this reason), and punishing Moscow's neoimperial behavior.[14]

POLICY PRESCRIPTION 12

Convert the energy revolution into lasting geopolitical gains.

The strategic premium the United States can gain from the unconventional energy boom is just as significant as the improvements seen in U.S. energy production.[15]

POLICY PRESCRIPTION 13

Meet the test of climate change.

Apart from including climate provisions more explicitly within trade agreements, the United States should also explore whether there is value in a new form of bilateral agreement, akin to a scaled-down free trade agreement or bilateral investment treaty.

POLICY PRESCRIPTION 14

Blunt the threat of state-sponsored geoeconomic cyberattacks.

The United States should create more intermediate costs to geoeconomic cyberattacks through two broad lines of effort. First, Washington should better empower private U.S. companies to engage in self-help, especially clarifying the rules surrounding defensive attacks (empowering companies to make their own decisions on whether to engage in so-called hackbacks, whereby companies hack into an attacker's computer, either to ascertain the damage of the initial attack or to nullify its benefits to the attacker). Second, to help to mitigate the sort of whack-a-mole quality that remedies can often assume (where exclusion from one market is remedied simply by shifting to other markets), the United States should work diplomatically to enact coordinated cyber measures, beginning with enacting binding measures between the United States and the European Union in the context of TTIP, and then expanding toward other major economies from there.

POLICY PRESCRIPTION 15

Reinforce economic foundations for democracy and peace in the Middle East and North Africa.

The United States should move immediately to articulate a mid- to long-term economic vision for the Middle East/North Africa region in order to strengthen U.S. power and influence there and to help stabilize these societies. For the past few years, as the Arab revolt has grown darker, the United States has by necessity focused on immediate stabilization, but with paltry results; a broader, longer-term vision can no longer wait, especially as the lack of such a vision is hampering our ability to manage the short-term challenges.

POLICY PRESCRIPTION 16

Refocus U.S. development aid toward cultivating the next generation of emerging markets, especially in Latin America and Africa.[16]

The Overseas Private Investment Corporation (OPIC), the U.S. government's primary private sector development partner, invested $2.58 billion in 2014 and returned $269 million to U.S. taxpayers (providing a net resource, as opposed to net expense, to the $56 billion international affairs budget).[17] OPIC is likely the most attractive and efficient foundation on which to build a robust U.S. development finance institution.

POLICY PRESCRIPTION 17

Shore up the rules governing geoeconomic playing fields.

Much as the General Agreement on Tariffs and Trade and the World Trade Organization offered a global solution to the problem of tariff barriers, the United States must develop a means of confronting the most salient forms of protectionism in evidence today, particularly when they are used for coercive purposes.

POLICY PRESCRIPTION 18

If America is going to be effective at exploiting its geoeconomic potential, it needs the right signals and bureaucratic structures in place, many of which can only come from the White House.

A new White House entity should be created and tasked with strengthening the country's overall understanding and use of geoeconomics and, as noted earlier, the harmonization of domestic and foreign policies. Housed within the National Security Council, this office should be staffed with roughly equal numbers of officials from the State, Intelligence, Defense, Treasury, and Commerce Departments, plus the Office of the U.S. Trade Representative, and should replace the current NSC International Economics Directorate.

POLICY PRESCRIPTION 19

Adopt new rules of engagement with Congress.

Aid budgets continue to shrink. Real questions hang over the fate in Congress of both TPP and TTIP. The G20 issued an ultimatum to the United States to implement changes, agreed in 2010, to voting weights and operations of the International Monetary Fund.[18] Add in Congress's refusal to renew the U.S. Export-Import Bank's license or reauthorize OPIC, and a dismaying picture emerges. Put bluntly, the U.S. Congress is often a serious impediment to implementing a coherent and comprehensive American geoeconomic strategy.

POLICY PRESCRIPTION 20

Increase university teaching around geoeconomics.

In order to produce the skills required over the long term to implement this ambitious geoeconomic agenda, academic preparation needs to go well beyond narrow disciplinary boundaries. Geoeconomics needs its own disciplinary language, one that joins the tools of economics with the logic of geopolitics.

The policy prescriptions contained in this chapter, if implemented in a sustained way, would make the United States a powerful geoeconomic actor in the world. They would allow the United States to address seriously the growing geoeconomic coercion practiced by authoritarian governments in Asia and Europe against their neighbors. They would give the industrial democracies new positive tools to influence regional and global geopolitics. And they would strengthen the U.S. alliance systems and thus bolster the current regional and global balance of power. But these measures will, of course, not be implemented in a day or, in many cases, even a year. They will require a fundamental redefinition of how America conducts its foreign policy, including in the first instance presidential leadership and an increased and sustained realization by the Congress that geoeconomic instruments can frequently promote America's national interests.

A Foreign Policy Centered on U.S. National Interests

The post-9/11 United States faces a blizzard of international problems: the rise of Chinese power, the return of Russian systemic destabilizing policies in Eurasia and beyond, chaos in the Middle East, the continuing danger of terrorism involving weapons of mass destruction (WMD). With statesmen rare in any age, perhaps it is best to return to a compelling compass for U.S. external behavior—American national interests as a basis for U.S. grand strategy—and to examine briefly again how geoeconomic instruments, as informed by history and enumerated in this book, might promote these interests.[19]

Vital national interests are conditions that are strictly necessary to safeguard and enhance Americans' survival and well-being in a free and secure nation. *Vital U.S. national interests are:* (1) preventing a WMD, major terrorist, or cyber attack on the American homeland; (2) maintaining the global balance of power, including through America's alliance systems, and preventing the emergence of a hegemonic rival on the Eurasian landmass; (3) ensuring the survival of U.S. allies and their active cooperation with the United States in shaping an international liberal order, based on democratic values and the rule of law, in which the United States can thrive; (4) preventing the emergence of hostile major powers or failed states on America's borders; and (5) ensuring the viability and stability of major global systems (trade, financial markets, supplies of energy, and the environment).

Extremely important national interests are conditions that, if compromised, would severely prejudice but not strictly imperil the ability of the U.S. government to safeguard and enhance the well-being of Americans in a free and secure nation. *Extremely important U.S. national interests are:* (1) preventing, deterring, and reducing the threat of the use of nuclear, biological, and chemical weapons anywhere; (2) preventing the regional proliferation of WMD and delivery systems; (3) promoting the acceptance of international rules of law and mechanisms for resolving or managing disputes peacefully; (4) promoting the well-being of U.S. allies and friends and protecting them from external aggression; (5) promoting democracy, prosperity, and stability in the Western Hemisphere; (6) preventing, managing, and (if possible at reasonable cost) ending major conflicts in important geographic regions; (7) maintaining a lead in key military-related and other strategic technologies, particularly information systems; and (8) preventing genocide.

U.S. military primacy continues to be essential in promoting and defending these national interests. With respect to international diplomacy, the United States is, as Secretary of State Madeleine Albright stressed, "the indispensable nation." At the same time, geoeconomic tools as defined and discussed in this volume seem especially relevant to each and every one of these vital and extremely important American national interests.

America's problem today is that after many decades of being preoccupied with the security dimension of American foreign policy, Washington instinctively reaches for the military instrument when often it is largely or entirely irrelevant or inappropriate to the external challenge at hand.

As we have earlier sought to demonstrate in detail, China, in our judgment, seeks a grand strategy that will end U.S. primacy in Asia and alter the balance of power in that vast and crucial region. And although the People's Republic of China is undertaking an ambitious program of military modernization, its tools in pursuing that grand strategy for the foreseeable future are primarily geoeconomic and not military.

The strength of the economies of America's Asian allies and of India will be crucial factors in their ability to resist Chinese economic coercion and to stand strong in maintaining the current balance of power in Asia writ large.

A stable and collaborative Egypt is a linchpin of broader U.S. national interests in the Middle East. Again, however, American military power will have little to do with whether Egypt overcomes its current monumental economic problems.

Tough international economic sanctions against Iran ultimately brought it to the negotiating table and to an agreement—a classic use of a geoeconomic instrument.

The future of Jordan—based in large part on the viability of its economy—will be an important determinant of whether the Middle East can regain a degree of peace and stability in the period ahead.

Putin's Russia appears to be embarked on an effort to re-create Soviet-era spheres of dominating influence on its borders and beyond, witness its military intervention in Syria. Although NATO allies in Eastern Europe in these circumstances require reassurance through U.S. military deployments and power projection, the future of Ukraine, Georgia, Azerbaijan, and the nations of Central Asia will not be decided by American military capabilities. The only hope for Ukraine to withstand Moscow's disruptive policies is to stabilize its economy, and that in turn depends extensively on American and European use of geoeconomic tools—trade, loans, grants—and the assistance of international lending institutions.

If Mexico's economic challenges were to produce deep and prolonged instability across the border, the United States certainly would be significantly diverted from its broader international missions and responsibilities.

During World War II, during most of the Cold War period and its aftermath, and in America's immediate responses after the 9/11 attacks, the military and security dimensions of U.S. foreign policy were rightly preeminent. After all, it was U.S. military power that defeated Germany and Japan, held NATO together, animated the U.S.-Japan alliance, deterred the Soviet Union, and killed most of al-Qa'ida's leadership. But in the years ahead, U.S. military prowess is not going to ease China's economic coercion against the nations of Asia, not going to help rescue Egypt, not going to promote Ukraine's independence from Moscow, and not going to assist Mexico to thrive as a stable modern democracy.

Either the United States will begin to use its geoeconomic power with much greater resolve and skill, or its national interests will increasingly be in jeopardy. U.S. domestic economic strength in the decades ahead must have more relevance to American national interests and the identification of consequent international threats and opportunities than simply funding a huge defense budget, useful as that is to U.S. global purposes. To recall Mao, international power and the influence needed to flourish and to shape the balance of power in America's favor must derive not only from the barrel of a gun but also from the strength and geopolitical applications of the U.S. economy. Whether administrations and the Congress will understand, digest, and implement this compelling reality with focus, clarity, and a sense of geoeconomic purpose remains a preeminent issue of American grand strategy in our era.

Robert Blackwill is Henry A. Kissinger senior fellow for U.S. foreign policy at the Council on Foreign Relations (CFR). Previously, Ambassador Blackwill served on the National Security Council (NSC) as deputy assistant to the president and deputy national security advisor for strategic planning under President George W. Bush, after serving as the U.S. ambassador to India from 2001 to 2003. He is the recipient of the 2007 Bridge-Builder Award for his role in transforming U.S.-India relations, and the 2016 Padma Bhushan Award from the government of India for distinguished service of a high order. Prior to reentering government in 2001, he was the Belfer lecturer in international security at Harvard University's Kennedy School of Government. During his fourteen years as a Harvard faculty member, he was executive dean of the Kennedy School, where he taught foreign and defense policy and public policy analysis. From 1989 to 1990, Ambassador Blackwill was special assistant to President George H.W. Bush for European and Soviet affairs, during which time he was awarded the Commander's Cross of the Order of Merit by the Federal Republic of Germany for his contribution to German unification. Earlier in his career, he served in a variety of government positions, including as U.S. ambassador to conventional arms negotiations with the Warsaw Pact and director for European affairs at the NSC. His newest book, *War by Other Means: Geoeconomics and Statecraft*, coauthored with Jennifer M. Harris, was published in April 2016 by Belknap Press, an imprint of Harvard University Press. He is a member of the Aspen Strategy Group.

Jennifer M. Harris is senior fellow at the Council on Foreign Relations. Prior to joining the Council, Harris was a member of the policy planning staff at the U.S. Department of State, responsible for global markets, geoeconomic issues, and energy security. In that role, Harris was a lead architect of Secretary of State Hillary Clinton's economic statecraft agenda, which launched in 2011. Before joining the State Department, Harris served on the staff of the U.S. National Intelligence Council, covering a range of economic and financial issues. Her work has appeared in the *New York Times; Foreign Affairs;* the *Washington Post,* and CNN, among other outlets. A Truman and a Rhodes scholar, she holds degrees in economics and international relations from Wake Forest University (BA) and the University of Oxford (MPhil), and a JD from Yale Law School. Harris is the author of *War By Other Means: Geoeconomics and Statecraft*, coauthored with Robert Blackwill and published by Belknap Press, an imprint of Harvard University Press, in 2016.

[1] Michael Mandelbaum, *The Road to Global Prosperity* (New York: Simon and Schuster, 2014), xvi–xvii.

[2] David Baldwin, *Economic Statecraft* (Princeton: Princeton University Press, 1985), 58–59.

[3] Ibid.

[4] Francis Fukuyama first presented the "end of history" thesis in 1989, arguing that there is a positive direction to current history, demonstrated by the collapse of authoritarian regimes of right and left and their replacement by liberal governments. In a later piece on the "future of history" he admits to having been a bit too quick off the mark. See "The End of History," *National Interest*, Summer 1989, and "The Future of History," *Foreign Affairs*, January/February 2012.

[5] Benn Steil and Robert Litan, "International Financial Statecraft," Council on Foreign Relations Special Report, August 2006.

[6] Members of the National Commission on Terrorist Attacks on the United States (9/11 Commission) gave the campaign against terrorist financing an A- in the commission's 2005 review of the implementation of its recommendations. That was the highest grade it gave for any aspect of the war on terrorism. For a discussion, see Council on Foreign Relations, "Terrorist Finance," 2002, http://www.cfr.org/publication.html?id=5080.

[7] Ibid.

[8] Author exchange with private sector commentator, May 2012.

[9] David Petraeus and Paras D. Bhayani, "North America: The Next Great Emerging Market? Capitalizing on North America's Four Interlocking Revolutions," John F. Kennedy School of Government, Harvard University, June 2015.

[10] See, e.g., Ben Bernanke, in his final speech as chairman of the Federal Reserve, "The Federal Reserve: Looking Back, Looking Forward," delivered at the annual meeting of the American Economic Association in Philadelphia, January 3, 2014. Richard Fisher, a conservative-leaning member of the U.S. Federal Reserve Board, argues, "The only thing holding the nation back from an economic boom was muddled fiscal policy"; Rob Curran, "Fisher Says Fed Has Overshot Mark on Stimulus," *Wall Street Journal*, October 10, 2014. See also "Global Financial Stability Report," International Monetary Fund, October 2014. Erskine Bowles, cochair of the bipartisan Simpson-Bowles Commission, reiterated that the 2011 sequester cuts to discretionary spending were counterproductive to the task of long-term debt and deficit reduction: "Instead of enacting a thoughtful, comprehensive fiscal plan that gradually reduced the deficit and put the budget on a fiscally sustainable long-term path, Washington allowed abrupt cuts from sequestration to take effect, harming the economic recovery and cutting important investments that could jeopardize future prosperity. And, for all that pain, the sequester does almost nothing to deal with the long-term drivers of our growing debt"; Erskine Bowles, "Urgency of Federal Deficit Remains," *USA Today*, October 27, 2014. See also Lawrence Summers, "Why Public Investment Really Is a Free Lunch," *Financial Times*, October 6, 2014.

[11] Michael Leachman and Chris Mai, "Most States Funding Schools Less than before the Recession," Center on Budget and Policy Priorities, May 20, 2014. Sheryll Poe, "The High Cost of Doing Nothing on Infrastructure Investment," U.S. Chamber of Commerce, September 23, 2014.

[12] U.S. Department of State, "The Department of State and USAID FY 2016 Budget," Bureau of Public Affairs fact sheet, February 23, 2015; Office of the Undersecretary of Defense (Comptroller), "United States Department of Defense Fiscal Year 2016 Budget Request: Overview," February 2015.

[13] These high aspirations were echoed by national security advisor Susan Rice at a White House press briefing: "White House Briefing on Obama Asia Trip with Questions on Ukraine," White House, Office of the Press Secretary, April 18, 2014.

[14] At a November 2014 exhibition of armored personnel carriers in Moscow, Mr. Putin observed how "you can do a lot more with weapons and politeness than just politeness," an unsubtle reference to the "polite" Russian soldiers who appeared in Crimea earlier that year. Central Asian and Eastern European nations are increasingly aware of the potential repercussions if Putin's Novorossiya is realized, and they are looking to the United States as an alternative to Russian and Chinese investment. For instance, securing closer trade and investment ties with the United States has been a primary focus of Kazakh foreign minister Erlan Idrissov's portfolio. "Putin's War of Words," *New York Times*, December 4, 2014 (quoting Putin). For more on Kazakhstan's efforts to increase economic ties with the United States, see generally "Joint Statement of the Third U.S.-Kazakhstan Strategic Partnership Dialogue," U.S. Department of State, December 10, 2014; Robert Guttman, "Kazakhstan Foreign Minister and U.S. Senior Officials Reaffirm and Strengthen Strategic Partnership," *TransAtlantic Magazine*, July 14, 2013.

[15] Many of these recommendations are from Meghan L. O'Sullivan, "North American Energy Remakes the Geopolitical Landscape: Understanding and Advancing the Phenomenon," Goldman Sachs, May 31, 2014.

[16] The current deficiencies of the U.S. Agency for International Development are explored in Christopher Holshek, "Why Is the United States Letting Its Best Foreign Aid Tool Fall Apart?," *Foreign Policy*, June 22, 2015.

[17] OPIC has returned money to U.S. taxpayers for thirty-seven straight years. See Overseas Private Investment Corporation, "OPIC 2014 Annual Report," www.opic.gov/sites/default/files/files/opic-fy14-annual-report.pdf. The Annual Management Report of the Overseas Private Investment Corporation for Fiscal Year 2014 put OPIC's 2014 investments at $2.96 billion with $358 million returned to the taxpayer. See, "Annual Management Report of the Overseas Private Investment Corporation for Fiscal Year 2014," OPIC, November 17, 2014, https://www.opic.gov/sites/default/files/files/fy2014-management-report.pdf.

[18] The changes would double the IMF's quota to $720 billion, shift six percentage points of total quota to emerging markets, and move two of the twenty-four IMF directorships from European to developing countries. See Robin Harding, "G20 Gives U.S. Ultimatum over IMF reform," *Financial Times*, April 11, 2014.

[19] Graham Allison and Robert Blackwill, *America's National Interests: A Report from the Commission on America's National Interests*, July 2000.

"If the system is designed to prevent change, then the system itself must change."

—JOHN DOWDY AND KIRK RIECKHOFF

Organizational Agility in Defense and National Security:
Elephants Learning to Dance

John Dowdy
Senior Partner
McKinsey & Company

Kirk Rieckhoff
Partner
McKinsey & Company

As the world continues to transform from the manufacturing economy of the industrial age to the digital economy of the information age, our national security organizations need to transform as well. This has been evident since at least 1999, when then-presidential hopeful George W. Bush said "today our military is still organized more for Cold War threats than for the challenges of a new century—for industrial age operations, rather than for information age battles."[1] American military forces have been, and continue to be, the most capable in the world, but our national security infrastructure, refined and perfected during the forty-plus years of the Cold War, is increasingly ill-suited to the challenges we face today.

Those challenges—increasing volatility, uncertainty, complexity, and ambiguity—are apparent to all, and even spawned a military acronym: VUCA. And yet our inherently bureaucratic national security institutions have failed to keep pace. The Department of Defense (DoD) is still largely governed by the Goldwater-Nichols Act of 1986, which focused more on procurement efficiency and unity of command than responsiveness. As a result, the system lacks the speed and agility needed to react to a rapidly changing world.

Similar changes are roiling the business world. But there, companies are successfully adapting by flattening their structures, leveraging modern information technology, and empowering managers to create flatter, faster-moving, and more flexible organizations. And although some would argue that these new-age management techniques don't apply to an organization as large and complex as the

Pentagon, in fact, they have been successfully deployed in numerous settings in the defense and security arena. In this chapter, we will examine the conditions that slow decision-making at the DoD and the techniques of organizational agility that, applied in ways that recognize the DoD's unique context, can get this behemoth on its feet and moving as fast as today's fluid conditions require.

Too Slow to Adapt

Today's Defense Department was largely shaped by the Goldwater-Nichols Act of 1986,[2] which sought to address operational shortcomings, including the failed Desert One rescue mission in Iran and widespread concerns about inefficiencies in the acquisition system. The structures, processes, and systems that resulted were like the body's slow-twitch muscles, well suited to the stable dynamics of the Cold War, but inadequate for the pivots and twists now required.

Government acquisition provides a powerful, strategically important example. Take the quest to secure Mine-Resistant Ambush Protected vehicles (MRAPs) to protect our forces from improvised explosive devices (IEDs) in Iraq and Afghanistan: When Robert M. Gates became defense secretary in 2006—describing his priorities as "Iraq, Iraq, and Iraq"—he was alarmed to see that the Pentagon was slow to provide protected mobility for soldiers, famously observing that the troops in Iraq and Afghanistan were operating on a war footing, but the Pentagon was not. By 2007, IEDs accounted for 69 percent of casualties and 63 percent of combat deaths in Iraq.[3] Protected vehicles were few and far between, limited to route clearance and explosive ordinance disposal. Worryingly, the Pentagon considered the MRAP just another in a long list of programs they were pursuing. In May 2007, Gates decided it should be run outside the calcified procurement system. MRAP production surged from 82 vehicles a month in June 2007 to 1,300 vehicles a month in December 2007.

The job of rushing MRAPs to Afghanistan for the troop surge in 2009 fell to then Under Secretary of Defense Ash Carter. Carter observed, "When the troops said they needed something, the response of the bureaucracy tended to be, 'Oh, we're making one of those. It'll be finished in 10 years. ... ' We can't take steps in 15-year increments."[4]

The lack of agility directly affects both the current and future strategic options available to leaders. The current acquisition portfolio contains solutions conceived in a very different world. More than twenty-five years after the dissolution of the Soviet Union in 1991, fully a quarter of spending relates to programs formulated during the

Cold War. Another 55 percent of spending relates to programs conceived after 1991 but before 9/11. Only 20 percent are post-9/11 in vintage. It certainly appears that there has been little reallocation of defense spending to reflect shifting threats.

The lack of agility extends across the national security apparatus. A government report on the 2012 attack on the U.S. consulate in Benghazi pointed to bureaucratic delays, criticizing the system for not being able to respond more quickly to the initial reports that the American diplomatic compound was under attack. Although it is now clear that help could not have arrived in time, the report notes that "despite President Obama and Secretary of Defense Leon Panetta's clear orders to deploy military assets, nothing was sent to Benghazi, and nothing was en route to Libya at the time the last two Americans were killed almost eight hours after the attacks began."[5]

Senator John McCain points to this lack of speed as a major issue: "We must face the uncomfortable fact that, too often, in too many cases, our enemies are getting the better of us. It is not that they are better led, or better equipped, or better positioned to succeed, or in possession of better strategies. In fact, the opposite is true. The problem, too often, is that we are simply too slow—too slow to adapt to changing circumstances, too slow to gain the initiative and maintain it, too slow to innovate, and too slow to do the vital work of strategic integration: marshaling the different functional elements of our defense organization to advance unified strategies, and implementing them effectively."[6]

Agility: The Real Third Offset

Many other organizations find themselves in the same position—but not all. According to Chris Donnelly, director of the Institute for Statecraft, while most institutions "have been unable to react and adapt fast enough to remain fit for purpose . . . [n]ot so a lot of the West's competitors. Countries like Russia and China—and sub-state actors like al-Qaeda or Islamic State—have learned more rapidly how to cope with today's instability, complexity, and rapid change. Our success in this competition will only be guaranteed if we learn to cope with change as they have."[7]

In his speech that served to launch the third offset strategy, Secretary of Defense Chuck Hagel set out his vision for coping with change. "Disruptive technologies and destructive weapons once solely possessed by only advanced nations have proliferated widely and are being sought or acquired by unsophisticated militaries and terrorist groups."[8] He therefore called upon the U.S. to seek a new means of "offsetting" enemy capabilities, as was done in early 1950s with nuclear weapons and again in the mid-1970s with stealth and precision-guided weapons. Both the first and second offsets primarily involved leveraging U.S. technology, and many have assumed that this will be the core of any third offset. But Secretary Hagel was clear that it won't be just about technology: "A third offset strategy will require innovative thinking, the development of new operational concepts, new ways of organizing, and long-term strategies."

Likewise, in a recent speech at the Brookings Institution, Senator McCain highlighted the need not just for new technology but for organizational change: "Instead of one great power rival, the United States now faces a series of trans-regional, cross-functional, multi-domain, and long-term strategic competitions that pose a significant challenge to the organization of the Pentagon and the military, which is often rigidly aligned around functional issues and regional geography."[9]

Lessons from the Private Sector

Meanwhile, similar ructions are taking place in the business world. Obviously, the precise changes confronting companies are different, but here too, VUCA is an apt term. The average lifespan of a company listed in the S&P 500 has decreased from sixty-seven years in the 1920s to just fifteen years today. Professor Richard Foster from Yale University found that on average an S&P 500 company is now being replaced every two weeks, and he estimates that 75 percent of current S&P 500 firms will be replaced by new firms by 2027.[10]

In business, massive upheaval is nothing new. In 1990, IBM had its most profitable year ever. By 1993, the company lost $16 billion, victimized by its lumbering size and an insular corporate culture. Many thought that Lou Gerstner joined IBM to preside over its break-up. Instead, he orchestrated a competitive and cultural transformation, as described in his book *Who Says Elephants Can't Dance?*

As disruptors upend markets, treaties dissolve, new regulations shift the rules, and talent is siphoned off by competitors, companies in every sector are either harnessing these forces or getting left behind. Winners are redesigning their strategies, rejiggering their operations, and getting closer to their customers. There is a thread that connects all of these efforts: a much more important role for cross-organizational teams, and a willingness to sidestep much of the established structure.

As they make these moves, companies are seeking the ideal qualities of agility—the ability to be both highly dynamic and inherently stable at the same time. It sounds paradoxical, and many organizations struggle with it, mistakenly thinking they only need to be faster. Those that manage to be both, organizations we call agile, are not only surviving but even thriving in this increasingly stressful world. As Nassim Nicholas Taleb wrote, these companies are the opposite of fragile: "The resilient resists shocks and stays the same; the antifragile gets better."[11]

Why are dynamism and stability the hallmarks of agility? Over the past fifteen years, McKinsey has developed and refined the Organizational Health Index (OHI) to assess the discrete elements of organizational effectiveness. The OHI dataset includes more than 1,100 public and private organizations, is global, and spans every major industry.[12] The healthiest companies (i.e., those in the top quartile) deliver returns to shareholders three times higher than the rest. Similar results are evident in the public sector.

When we studied speed and stability, we found that organizations had widely varying capabilities (Exhibit 1).[13] Relatively few stood out as being especially agile: 58 percent of them had speed, stability, or both that hovered near average. Eight percent were fast but not stable, similar to the now-familiar start-ups that have pervaded all areas of business. An additional 22 percent of organizations were either slow and unstable, a group we describe as trapped (14 percent), or slow and stable, which we call bureaucratic (the remaining 8 percent).

Twelve percent of our sample were agile: organizations that are both quick and stable. Intriguingly, these organizations were 70 percent more likely to be in the top quartile of organizational health than others (Exhibit 2). The bureaucratic organizations—and though we have not surveyed the DoD, we think it would probably qualify as one—have by far the poorest organizational health of the three non-agile types.

Exhibit 1

Few companies excelled in either relative speed or stability— 58 percent hovered near average.

Distribution of 161 companies by Organizational Health Index (OHI) scores[1]

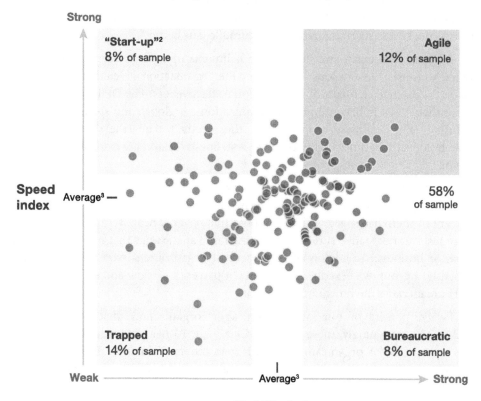

Speed index

Strong

"Start-up"[2]
8% of sample

Agile
12% of sample

Average[3] —

58%
of sample

Trapped
14% of sample

Bureaucratic
8% of sample

Weak — Average[3] — Strong

Stability index

[1]Scores have been adjusted to remove the portion of OHI variance shared by the factors of speed and stability, to highlight the specific contribution of each factor (speed or stability) along its axis.
[2]That is, companies with a mode of operating suited to a very small start-up (not actual start-ups).
[3]Mean +/− 0.50 standard deviation on each axis of matrix.

McKinsey&Company

Exhibit 2

Seventy percent of agile companies rank in the top quartile of organizational health.

% of organizations within each category, by quartile, for Organizational Health Index (OHI) scores[1] (n = 161)

■ Top quartile   ■ Second quartile   ■ Third quartile   ▪ Bottom quartile

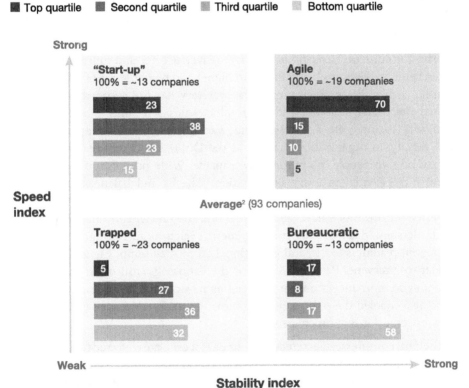

Note: Figures may not sum to 100%, because of rounding.

[1]Scores have been adjusted to remove the portion of OHI variance shared by the factors of speed and stability, to highlight the specific contribution of each factor (speed or stability) along its axis.
[2]Mean +/− 0.50 standard deviation on each axis of matrix; these 93 companies were nearly evenly spread across quartiles for organizational health.

McKinsey&Company

Resistance Is Feudal

Of course organizations are by no means monolithic, and some parts can be much healthier and agile than others. Certainly, exogenous conditions (e.g., the authorities given to the U.S. Special Operations Command) contribute to differences in performance. However the vast preponderance of variation comes from three internal forces of resistance: the desire for control, organizational complexity, and a cultural aversion to risk. A troubling mindset that sees the organization as a machine underlies all three.

Desire for control. Layering of management structures and functional silos can often result in decisions being forced to higher and higher levels of management. Within each military service, only the secretary has the authority to integrate across functional, mission, and geographic issues. The only officials with the authority to integrate across separate warfighting domains are the secretary and deputy. In organizations as vast as the DoD, that is an impossible burden to put on two people, no matter how capable. Without question some level of control is essential in every organization. Checks and balances, independent reviews, and governance bodies all work to improve decisions. However, national security organizations have gone far beyond the efficient frontier. A profusion of leadership "dashboards," tracking metrics such as recruiting yields, budget data, unit readiness levels, and operational activity, all tempt the action-oriented leader to intervene. Peter W. Singer of the Brookings Institution observed that "although commanders are empowered as never before, the new technologies have also enabled the old trends of command interference, even taking them to new extremes of micromanagement."[14]

Unhelpful complexity. Secretary of Defense Robert Gates referred to the Pentagon as "the largest and most complex organization on the planet."[15] Few would argue. And the problems of complexity are well known: simply put, it makes it harder for individuals to get things done. But isn't complexity part and parcel of being big? Yes and no. Research suggests that some complexity is essential and value-adding (e.g., the range of missions, geography), some is imposed (e.g., federal law), but what remains is largely dysfunctional, self-imposed, and worth reevaluating.[16] Federal acquisition regulations, for example, have become so complex that the Air Force is considering building an artificial intelligence system to navigate the thousands of pages of rules and policies.

Cultural aversion to risk. Behavioral economics has demonstrated that humans weigh risk twice as heavily as a similar benefit.[17] Individuals worry about being wrong, making a superior angry, or alienating other parts of the organization. Without an imperative to act (such as the profit motive in the private sector), individuals rationally seek ever more information, conduct additional analysis, build consensus, await direction or permission, or optimize for those most important to them (their "tribe") rather than the enterprise. This often results in lowest common denominator recommendations to senior leaders—what former Undersecretary of Defense for Policy Michele Flournoy calls "the tyranny of consensus."[18] Only when the organization must respond to a crisis will individuals stick their neck out. As mission needs surge, the risk of inaction is no longer acceptable, entrepreneurialism and best-effort judgment are rewarded, and errors become expected, accepted, and corrected. A common refrain we have heard from national security executives is, "I wish my organization could perform all the time like it does in a crisis."

Man vs. Machine—A Blocking Mindset

Influenced by Frederick Taylor's and Max Weber's powerful ideas, propounded roughly a century ago, many large organizations still think their organizations should operate like a well-oiled machine whose working parts fit together seamlessly. In this machine view, bureaucracy is prized, as it results in routine, repetitive, orderly action, with clear boundaries and an established hierarchy for oversight. When decisions require coordination, committees bring together leaders to share information and to review proposals. All processes are designed in a precise, deliberate way to ensure that employees can rely on rules, handbooks, and instructions to execute tasks.

Today's problem is that by the time organizations have designed this kind of structure, the world has already moved on, and it's time to change again. In a 2015 McKinsey survey, more than half of the executives surveyed said their companies are making significant structural changes, at either the unit or the enterprise level, as frequently as every two or three years. The redesigns often take one or two years to complete. Unsurprisingly, only 23 percent of the redesigns were deemed successful by respondents. The rest failed, in part because they designed solutions to problems that were already passé. The machine view has much to offer: logic, consistency, predictability. But if success relies on responding to the unpredictable, this approach results in almost constant disruption and change fatigue.

What Does Organizational Agility Look Like?

The ability to be both stable and dynamic, the essence of true organizational agility, can be seen through a simple product analogy—the smartphone. Smartphones have become ubiquitous in large part because of their design and functionality. The hardware and operating system form a stable foundation. On top of this sits a dynamic application layer where new apps can be added, updated, modified, and deleted over time as requirements change and new capabilities develop.

In the same way, agile companies design their organizations with a backbone of stable elements, for example a simple top-level organizational structure or a common way of doing things that everyone follows. These foundations, like a smartphone's hardware and operating system, are likely to endure. Agile companies also have dynamic capabilities: organizational "apps" to plug in as new opportunities arise or unexpected challenges threaten to destabilize formerly protected profit streams. In the national security space, agile would provide a stable framework within which dynamic cross-functional teams are formed, nurtured, and dissolved. Instead, today these "apps" exist outside the system or become a permanent part of it (e.g., task forces, special offices, and new governance committees).

Our work has highlighted three core areas where agile organizations excel: organizational structure, which defines how resources are distributed; processes, which determine how things get done; and people.

Structure. Agile organizations set a stable, simple structure as their backbone. The top team comprises the leaders of the missions and core functions, with mission leaders typically deciding how budget is allocated. The dynamic dimension is built from modular teams. The teams have clear missions with autonomy to make decisions and are charged with end-to-end ownership of a process with a clear customer (or, in the national security context, with mission outcomes). Firms such as ING, Google, and Siemens use this structure to great effect. These units can come in many different sizes, mission sets, and capabilities; they are the "apps" of the organization.

Process. Agile organizations keep their operations stable by underpinning the way they work with a standardized, minimally specified set of core processes. These are usually "signature" processes—the essential activities at which the company must excel in order to win. These processes are often hard for competitors to replicate, providing sustained competitive advantage. In a brand- and innovation-driven consumer-goods company, such as P&G, for example, product development and external communication are high on the list of signature processes. Amazon's synchronized supply chain, with its common language and standards identifying clear decision rights and handoffs, is another.

People. No matter the structure or processes in place, people ultimately accomplish the mission. People crave stability and find it in the common values that hold the organization together. If the values are truly embodied in the organization, they provide a strong shared culture and purpose. But people also crave the new, and organizations can tap that to improve their dynamism. Agile organizations focus on creating strong internal motivation and passion, a culture of self-improvement and stretch, and an atmosphere of open, honest feedback.

Elephants Learning to Dance

Changing the way the Pentagon operates in an increasingly complex, multi-threat environment has been intoned so often that it is widely regarded as a truism in defense circles. The real question is how to do it. Stephen Rosen, one of the leading thinkers on innovation and the modern military, summarized the problem well when he said: "Almost everything we know in the theory about large bureaucracies suggests not only that they are hard to change, but that they are *designed not to change*."[19] If the system is designed to prevent change, then the forces at work in the system must be changed. Below are three actions that can disarm the forces of resistance, and increase the agility of our national security apparatus:

1. Lower decision-making time to within our adversaries' OODA (observe, orient, decide, and act) loop. In May 2012, Major General H.R. McMaster admitted: "We have a perfect record in predicting future wars—right? ... And that record is 0 percent."[20] Given our inability to predict the future, success depends on being able to react fast enough to effectively cope with the unexpected. To reduce the cycle time, each organization should identify its signature decision-making processes (e.g., resource allocation, requirement-to-fielding, deployment training) and start from a blank slate. In our experience, making incremental adjustments to established processes rarely works, as it leads inexorably to a prolonged internal battle. The organization should use as few steps as possible and no more than can fit within the required timeline. Most importantly, the number of reviews must be drastically shrunk to only those that can significantly improve the answer. Doing this will unwind the massive, self-imposed complexity of many of the current processes. For example, in our view, the planning, programming, budgeting, and execution (PPBE) cycle should be shortened from 30 months to 12—or, better, might even be made obsolete.

One example of a fundamental transformation of organizational agility comes from the Joint Special Operations Task Force (JSOTF), which was commanded by General Stanley McChrystal and sent to Iraq to kill or capture Abu Musab al-Zarqawi, the leader of al-Qaeda in Iraq. In its early days, JSOTF found itself outmaneuvered by a more agile adversary that was organized more like a network than a hierarchy and leveraged modern communications technology. General McChrystal observed that "the wickets through which decisions had to pass made even the most efficient manifestation of our system unacceptably slow."[21] He "discarded a century of management wisdom and pivoted from a pursuit of mechanical efficiency to organic adaptability."[22] The mission, as is well known, was a success.

2. Control that which adds significant value, and let go of the rest. As described earlier, the current national security system has a massive number of controls in place, all individually well intended, but in aggregate they create a system that struggles under its own weight. The controls manifest in three ways: policies (including regulations, instructions, and laws); governance; and hierarchy.

To become agile, the controls need to be rationalized. The policy aspect is likely the most complex and requires a "clean-sheet" review, with the goal of defining only the minimum specifications needed to ensure interoperability. Governance bodies should be consolidated, creating single decision points. And the hierarchical reviews of decisions along the chain of command should be cut to a single one. In our experience, many more decisions can be safely made by the responsible end-to-end unit, as we discuss next, and not by top leadership.

3. Build end-to-end mission units, embed the enterprise view into each, and link and support them as needed. In the quest for efficiency and in an effort to minimize individual risk, many national security organizations have organized along functional lines, with no single unit having end-to-end accountability, resulting in a lack of responsiveness. What's needed now is a structure of many self-contained units, each with a clear mission, distinct accountability for performance of the mission, and the resources and access to expertise necessary to execute. The private sector calls the largest of these organizations business units; the smallest versions are called integrated product teams.

Agile organizations typically decouple the formal reporting structure (organization chart and functions) from the daily work management and the professional development of people. Their driving principle is to build the teams and individual work around meaningful end-to-end streams of work with a clear mission and direct results. The DoD has many excellent examples of high-performing business units and, especially, smaller self-contained teams. In the national security arena, the various missions determine the core end-to-end processes. All aspects of accomplishing a mission (such as training, acquisition, and execution) are managed by this unit. Functional processes (recruiting, finance, IT, and so on) provide support to the end-to-end units. Just as crucially, agile organizational processes include full transparency on performance and mission outcomes. Examples of this exist already, but most are on the operational side. The Marine Corps has Marine Expeditionary Units, the Army has Brigade Combat Teams, the Navy has Carrier Battle Groups, and the Air Force has Air Expeditionary Forces. But in the intelligence arena and the entire support side, most functions are siloed, with mission responsibility only coming together at the agency director or service secretary level.

In the modern era, the enterprise view can be pushed further down into the organization, enabling units to make fast, efficient decisions based on their in-depth knowledge of both the frontline situation and the impact on the enterprise. Modeling can often clarify the complex system interactions with the enterprise. Providing units access to the relevant "big picture" lets them make choices that align with the broader goals.

Another Vector of Change: Congress Reconsiders Goldwater-Nichols

Recent reforms, including a set of acquisition reforms advanced by Secretary of Defense Ash Carter and Under Secretary of Defense for Acquisition, Technology, and Logistics Frank Kendall, have all been made, naturally enough, in the context of the existing policy structure. But a consensus is emerging that that structure—the processes and authorities adopted in line with the Goldwater-Nichols Act of 1986— needs a refresh in order to bolster America's military dominance.[23]

A new series of reforms is underway as part of the National Defense Authorization Act, with competing versions emerging from the House and Senate Armed Service Committees. As the House and Senate begin the process of reconciling vastly different defense policy bills, they are considering a number of proposals to create nimbler military commands. The current Senate version would require the secretary of defense to create a series of cross-functional mission teams to integrate across regions, functions, and domains, with representatives from policy, intelligence, acquisition, budget, and the services. The differences between the House and Senate bills will be ironed out in conference before the final version of the bill goes to the president before the end of the fiscal year on September 30th. As these reforms progress, the DoD will surely watch closely and may be spurred to action. A program of internally designed reforms will likely be more effective than a set of legislative changes imposed upon the DoD.

The Other Animals at the Dance: Reform Beyond the Pentagon

Although reform to the Pentagon is arguably necessary, it would be wrong to think that threats to American national security can be addressed by focusing on DoD alone. Harlan Ullman argues: "The United States has the finest and arguably the most competent military in the world. Two wars in Iraq and one in Afghanistan, as well as dozens of smaller engagements have been competently and often brilliantly conducted by the U.S. military. Failure was not due to the shortcomings of the American military. Too often, the U.S. military became the surrogate for the inability to provide a 'comprehensive' or whole-government approach to resolving crucial political problems."[24] National security reform must go beyond the Pentagon.

Adjustments to the new world are already taking place elsewhere in the national security space. Senator McCain has pointed to reforms to overcome similar challenges at the National Counterterrorism Center, the Joint Special Operations Command, the National Security Agency, and the CIA.[25] Although details are appropriately sparse, the CIA has said that it embarked on a sweeping restructuring earlier this year that will bring an end to divisions that have been in place for decades, creating 10 new centers that team analysts with operators. The overhaul is designed to foster deeper collaboration and an intensified focus on a range of security issues and threats, replacing long-standing divisions that cover the Middle East, Africa, and other regions with hybrid "mission centers" modeled on the CIA's Counterterrorism Center.[26] Similar changes can and should be replicated across the national security arena.

· · ·

Warren Bennis, widely regarded as a pioneer of the contemporary field of leadership studies, said it well: Success in management requires learning as fast as the world is changing.

John Dowdy is a Senior Partner in the London office of McKinsey & Company, where he leads the Firm's global Defense and Security practice. Mr. Dowdy has conducted more than 100 projects on defense and security issues in eight different countries over his 26 year McKinsey career. He has worked extensively in countries including the U.S., the U.K., Denmark, Australia, Japan and Canada. Over the past decade, he has been involved in projects improving the efficiency and effectiveness of Air, Land and Maritime forces, headquarters organization, defense supply chain and logistics processes, and counter terrorism, among others. Most recently, he led McKinsey's support to the Equipment Support Plan (ESP) Review in the UK, which delivered £2.5 billion in audited savings. Mr. Dowdy leads McKinsey's research on best practices in defense. He led McKinsey's benchmarking on the efficiency and effectiveness of 33 defense forces around the world. He is a fellow at the Royal United Services Institute (RUSI), where he serves as a member of the Board of Trustees. Mr. Dowdy holds an MBA with high distinction from Harvard Business School, where he graduated as a George F. Baker scholar, and a B.S. in Electrical Engineering and Computer Science with honors from the University of California at Berkeley. He is a private pilot.

Kirk Rieckhoff is a Partner in McKinsey & Company's Washington DC Office, where he has worked primarily in the areas of strategy and organizational design. Select experience includes: developing business unit strategy; diagnosing contract overruns; developing the strategy for a major U.S. Defense Service, where he worked with top leadership for each of their major missions to identify and prioritize the critical choices facing the service; improving government performance in Iraq – working to improve the performance of their state owned enterprises (SOEs); supply chain redesign; and, organization redesign - redesigning the parts procurement organization for a large manufacturer. Prior to joining McKinsey, Mr. Rieckhoff was a fighter pilot in the U.S. Air Force for 13 years. His service included combat missions in both the Iraq and Afghanistan conflicts, earning the Silver Star. Additionally he deployed multiple times throughout the PACOM AOR. In his last tour he served directly for the Chief of Staff of the Air Force as speechwriter and handling special projects. Mr. Rieckhoff has a B.S. in Aeronautical Engineering from the U.S. Air Force Academy, a Master's in Public Policy from Harvard School of Government, and a Master's in Organizational Management from George Washington University.

[1] George W. Bush. September 23, 1999. "A Period of Consequences," at The Citadel.

[2] Goldwater–Nichols Department of Defense Reorganization Act of 1986, Pub.L. 99–433.

[3] Atkinson, Rick. September 30, 2007. "The Single Most Effective Weapon Against Our Deployed Forces." *Washington Post*, graphic titled "More Attacks, Mounting Casualties: The Toll." http://www.washingtonpost.com/wp-dyn/content/graphic/2007/09/28/GR2007092802161.html

[4] Carter, Ashton. February 4, 2015. Testimony before the Senate Armed Services Committee.

[5] Report of the Select Committee on the Events Surrounding the 2012 Terrorist Attack in Benghazi. June 28, 2016.

[6] McCain, John. June 28, 2016. Opening statement at hearing on Improving Strategic Integration at the Department of Defense.

[7] Donnelly, Chris. June/July 2016. "Success Needs a Military Mentality." *The World Today*. See also Donnelly, Chris. June 2016. "War in Peacetime: Coping with Today's Rapidly Changing World." The Institute for Statecraft.

[8] Hagel, Chuck. September 3, 2014. "Defense Innovation Days," Opening Keynote. Southeastern New England Defense Industry Alliance, Newport, RI.

[9] The Brookings Institution. May 2016. "New Demands on the Military and the 2017 National Defense Authorization Act."

[10] Foster, Richard. 2015. *Creative Destruction Whips Through Corporate America*. Boston: Innosight.

[11] Taleb, Nassim Nicholas. November 27, 2012. *Antifragile: Things That Gain From Disorder*. New York: Random House.

[12] www.ohisolution.com

[13] Bazigos, Michael, Aaron De Smet, and Chris Gagnon. December 2015. "Why agility pays." *McKinsey Quarterly*.

[14] Singer, Peter W. July 2009. *Tactical Generals: Leaders, Technology, and the Perils*. Washington, DC: Brookings Institution.

[15] Gates, Robert M. 2016. *A Passion for Leadership*. New York: Knopf.

[16] Birkinshaw, Julian, and Suzanne Heywood. May 2010. "Putting Organizational Complexity in Its Place." *McKinsey Quarterly*.

[17] Kahneman, Daniel. 1992. "Advances in Prospect Theory: Cumulative Representation of Uncertainty." *Journal of Risk and Uncertainty*.

[18] Flournoy, Michèle A. December 8, 2015. "The Urgent Need for Defense Reform." Testimony before the Senate Armed Services Committee.

[19] Rosen, Stephen Peter. 1991. *Winning the Next War*. Ithaca, NY: Cornell University Press.

[20] Feith, David. May 11, 2012. "H.R. McMaster: The Warrior's-Eye View of Afghanistan." *Wall Street Journal*.

[21] McChrystal, Stanley. 2015. *Team of Teams: New Rules of Engagement for a Complex World*. New York: Portfolio.

[22] Mcchrystal, Stanley. February 2011. "It Takes a Network: The New Front Line of Modern Warfare." *Foreign Policy*.

[23] Rodriguez, Stephen, and Don Mathis. June 2016. "First World Problem: Defense Acquisition and the Competition for Ideas." *War on the Rocks*.

[24] Ullman, Harlan. March 28, 2016. "National Security Reform Must go Beyond Pentagon." UPI.

[25] McCain, John. June 28, 2016. Opening statement at hearing on Improving Strategic Integration at the Department of Defense.

[26] Miller, Greg. March 6, 2015. "CIA Plans Major Reorganization and a Focus on Digital Espionage." *Washington Post*.

Part 5

SUMMARY AND CONCLUDING THOUGHTS

CHAPTER 15

ASG 2016 Wrap up

Peter Feaver
Duke University

"The next president is inheriting a geopolitical mess, with the public exhausted and perhaps unwilling to support what needs to be done and a world eagerly hoping that the next administration will repair broken relations around the world and America's reputation."

—PETER FEAVER

ASG 2016 Wrap up

Peter Feaver
Professor of Political Science and Public Policy
Duke University

The ASG Summer Workshop 2016 covered essentially the same topics that we explored in Summer Workshop 2008—the last time we had a certain presidential transition looming. Comparing across those two sessions, I found three important themes that we can take away from this year's session.

Theme 1: Déjà Vu All Over Again

There are striking similarities in the kinds of critiques and recommendations that the workshop participants flagged in 2008 and again in 2016. That is partly good news but mostly bad news. Partly good news in that we were able to quickly achieve a wide degree of bipartisan consensus on the things that were deficient in the national security architecture and the kinds of reforms we would like to see. Mostly bad news in that it is the same laundry list of problems and proposed reforms. Clearly, when it came to managing national security, as a country, we did not make the progress the ASG Summer Workshop 2008 hoped to foster.

Four items from the 2008 to-do list have eerie echoes in 2016.

1.   In 2008, we agreed that the National Security Council (NSC) was too large, consisted of too much micromanaging, and needed to be made more strategic. Moreover, we agreed that all the strategic planning the country needed to do could not be done from the White House, especially not with only a three- to four-person strategic planning group on the NSC staff. (In 2008, I made the parochial point that, notwithstanding this critique, there were better strategic planning results from the U.S. government when there was a well-functioning and empowered strategic planning cell—even a small group—at the White House, than if there is no such cell and the planning is left solely to the departments. But that view might have been dismissed as special pleading from me given that I ran that office.)

2. In 2008, Tony Blinken wrote a persuasive paper for the group lamenting how poor executive-congressional relations were under the preceding eight years and assuring us that the next administration would have much better outreach down Pennsylvania Avenue.

3. In 2008, there was a strong bipartisan consensus calling for an increase in civilian capacity to rectify the imbalance with the Department of Defense (DoD). Many 2008 workshop participants lamented how DoD's outsized role had militarized foreign policy.

4. Crucially, the looming geopolitical context participants described this summer is precisely the one we fretted about in 2008. The next president is inheriting a geopolitical mess, with the public exhausted and perhaps unwilling to support what needs to be done and a world eagerly hoping that the next administration will repair broken relations around the world and America's reputation. This is almost a verbatim repeat of 2008.

One important difference between 2008 and 2016: there were more flights of grandiosity in 2008 promising major change. Perhaps we have been chastened by the experience and frustration of the last eight years. Consider just one example: if former Secretary of Defense Robert Gates, former Secretary of State Hillary Clinton, and a Democratic supermajority in Congress cannot rebalance State and the DoD, then it will likely not be radically rebalanced in our lifetime. The best we can hope for may be incremental change. Some humility in this area may be salutary because of my Iron Law of Interagency Reform (with apologies to Longfellow): "Whom the gods would destroy, they first convince to embark on a Goldwater Nichols of the Interagency." Many of the action items from this year's workshop were more granular and practical than in 2008, suggesting that experts in both parties may have been chastened by experience.

To be sure, the 2016 Workshop did highlight some areas of institutional progress. We heard compelling cases for how the Department of Homeland Security and the Department of Commerce are better integrated into the national security architecture than they were eight years ago. Recently, the administration did launch some NSC reform efforts that will be useful to continue and expand in the next administration.

However, there is much more continuity in the critique between 2008 and 2016 than one would expect, which leads to two central questions:

(i) Why does it seem like so little progress has been made on the issue of reform? Why didn't the current administration adopt the measures the panel recommended previously?

(ii) What makes experts, officials, and policy makers like us think we can do better this time?

Theme 2: Political Context

How can we undertake the larger reforms we discussed without a galvanizing crisis? In fact, some of the reforms we talked about run contrary to the rising tide of populism; if the tide does not recede, it could undermine the architecture faster than we can repair it. How do we win America, which we need to win before we can win the world?

In 2008, there was such a crisis, the financial crisis, and it produced a new president with supermajorities in both the Senate and the House of Representatives. There are dueling partisan narratives of what came next. The Democrat narrative is that President Obama's sincere efforts at bipartisan reform and compromise were rebuffed by Republicans gripped by the fever of hyper-partisanship. The Republican narrative is that President Obama followed Rahm Emanuel's advice and turned the crisis into an opportunity to do a host of other things that were not necessarily on the ASG agenda.

We do not need to resolve these dueling narratives to see the most important point for our present situation: the new president is not going to have the luxury, if we can call it that, of the political clout that comes from a galvanizing crisis. There is a chance that in the November 2016 elections, the Democrats will narrowly win the Senate and, in extreme scenarios, also the House. Even if the Democrats sweep both the executive and legislative branches, there is little likelihood that Hillary Clinton will have the perceived mandate that Obama had in 2009. The reform issues we discussed in Summer Workshop 2016 were not debated in the Democratic primary, and Donald Trump did not raise them in the general election. Instead, it is much more likely that if there is a crisis, it will be a crisis of political legitimacy, with whomever wins the White House starting out as the most unpopular incoming president in modern times—perhaps much less than the 57 percent approval rating that President George W. Bush started with, and he, as we all remember, started out under the cloud of the Florida recount controversy.

How does this crisis of political legitimacy constrain or shape the debate over institutional reform? This summer we only scratched the surface of this thorny question.

This summer we rightly and repeatedly emphasized that personnel are the key that unlocks policy and organizational effectiveness. Yet we did not apply that insight as thoroughly as we should have. The discussion was very theoretical, when in fact we have a pretty good idea as to what kind of person will be the next U.S. president. In fact, we can narrow it down to two very distinctive types of personality. If so, then we should have applied what we know about the traits of the two presidential candidates to the specific institutional reforms we were debating. Which design features would work best for this candidate versus that candidate? Would Hillary Clinton opt for and/or benefit from a White House-centric system? What steps could we take to mitigate her known weaknesses and maximize her known strengths? Such personality-specific designing is much harder to do for Donald Trump, but also much more important.

And what about the truly novel aspect of the current political context: the fact that a large fraction of the foreign policy human capital within the Republican party has disavowed the Republican nominee? How do we mitigate the downside of the #NeverTrump movement, which has made it harder to build out a national security team for President Trump? Perhaps it matters less who is appointed for the core policy areas he cares about, since, based on his campaign, he seems especially reluctant to delegate to staff members or rely on their advice. But there are lots of areas he does not care as much about that might in fact be run by permanent government officials or an unpredictable political appointee. If there is a President Trump, would not the highest priority coming out of the deliberations of the ASG Summer Workshop 2016 be helping him assemble the best team he can? After all, personnel are the key to policy effectiveness.

Such scenario-based planning should go beyond personalities to factor in intra-party political constraints. Consider one illustrative example: How would President Clinton find the money to keep the "third offset strategy" going? The third offset strategy is an anathema to Democratic doves, and may be a hard sell even to Democratic hawks outside the DoD. How plausible is it that a politically constrained President Clinton could spend the political capital to move this strategy along when she looks over her left shoulder and sees an impossible wish list from Democratic congressional allies and then looks over her right shoulder and sees a frustrated Republican party disinclined to compromise?

Theme 3: Other Barking Dogs?

Finally, despite covering an impressive portion of the national security waterfront, we left some important topics unaddressed. We paid inadequate attention to civil-military relations. Relations between senior civilian and senior military leaders are under quite a bit of strain now—more so than in 2008—and the natural stress that comes from transitioning between administrations will only increase the strain. And that is if the transition is a normal one, when hardly anything about the 2016 election cycle has been normal.

Additionally, there is a longstanding Aspen Strategy Group tradition we must recognize: there will likely be some sort of surprise this fall that was not anticipated by our workshop agenda. In 2008, it was the Russian invasion of Georgia and the fall of Lehman House. In 2014, it was a near-death experience for Erbil. What will it be this year? North Korea? A domestic political crisis? Will that crisis upend reform efforts, or could it be the opportunity that an adroit president can leverage?

Looking to the future, there are three urgent tasks that fall squarely within the ASG mandate. First, what can we do to help repair the breaches within the Republican party, particularly over national security? Second, how do we deal with the Bernie Sanders and Elizabeth Warren wing of the Democratic party? Lastly, how do we repair bipartisanship? What are obligations for the party that is out of power? What are the obligations for the party in power? What are the obligations of outside groups like the Aspen Strategy Group?

I conclude with one final comparison between the 2016 and 2008 workshops. In 2008, there was a general sense that Obama enjoyed the most favorable electoral prospects, so discussions about "what the next administration should do" were thinly veiled discussions about "what we hope Obama will do." The electoral picture is a bit murkier in 2016, but, certainly during the August session, the Clinton campaign seemed to hold the whip hand and this was reflected in our discussions ("The next president, she. . . ."). But even in August, the possibility of a Trump victory was higher than many other high-impact contingencies we considered. And since our workshop, the race has tightened even further. Has our group seriously weighed what must be considered a plausible contingency: What would we do if Trump wins?

Peter D. Feaver is a Professor of Political Science and Public Policy at Duke University. He is Director of the Triangle Institute for Security Studies and Director of the Duke Program in American Grand Strategy. From June 2005 to July 2007, Dr. Feaver served as Special Advisor for Strategic Planning and Institutional Reform on the National Security Council Staff at the White House, where his responsibilities included the national security strategy, regional strategy reviews, and other political-military issues. In 1993-94, he served as Director for Defense Policy and Arms Control on the National Security Council at the White House, where his responsibilities included the national security strategy review, counterproliferation policy, regional nuclear arms control, and other defense policy issues. Dr. Feaver is author of *Armed Servants* (Harvard, 2003) and of *Guarding the Guardians* (Cornell, 1992). He is co-author: with Christopher Gelpi and Jason Reifler, of *Paying the Human Costs of War* (Princeton, 2009); with Susan Wasiolek and Anne Crossman, of *Getting the Best Out of College* (Ten Speed Press, 2008, 2nd edition 2012); and with Christopher Gelpi, of *Choosing Your Battles* (Princeton, 2004). He is co-editor, with Richard H. Kohn, of *Soldiers and Civilians* (MIT, 2001). He has published numerous other monographs, scholarly articles, book chapters, and policy pieces on grand strategy, American foreign policy, public opinion, nuclear proliferation, civil-military relations, and cybersecurity. He blogs at shadow.foreignpolicy.com, and is a Contributing Editor to *Foreign Policy* magazine. He received a Ph.D from Harvard University. He is a member of the Aspen Strategy Group.